THE LEGAL ROAD BLOCKS TO A NLRBE

(NATURAL LAW RESOURCE-BASED ECONOMY)

IN THE CASE OF
LEGAL REALITY VS LAWFUL LIVING

www.roadblocksnlrbe.com

The Legal Roadblocks to a NLRBE
Legal Reality Vs Lawful Living

1st Edition 2017

"To be governed is to be watched, inspected, spied upon, directed, law-driven, numbered, regulated, enrolled, indoctrinated, preached at, controlled, checked, estimated, valued, censured, commanded by creatures who neither the right nor the wisdom nor the virtue to do so. To be governed is to be at every operation, at every transaction noted, registered, counted, taxed, stamped, measured, numbered, assessed, licensed, authorized, admonished, prevented, forbidden, reformed, corrected, punished. It is, under pretext of public utility and in the name of the general interest, to be placed under contribution, drilled,fleeced, exploited, monopolized, extorted from, squeezed, hoaxed, robbed; then, at the slightest resistance, the first word of complaint, to be repressed, fined, vilified, harassed, hunted down, abused, clubbed, disarmed, bound, choked, imprisoned, judged, condemed, shot, deported, sacrificed, sold, betrayed; and to crown all, mocked, ridiculed, derided, outraged, dishonored. That is government; that is it's justice; that is it's morality

Pierre – Joseph Proudhon

CONTENTS

SECTION ONE - THE HISTORY

i

SECTION TWO - THE CIRCUMSTANCE

SECTION THREE - THE REALITY

ACKNOWLEDGEMENTS

In no particular order a big thanks to one and all of the following for their knowledge and teachings in all their endeavours, and campaigns of exposition: either ongoing or everlasting, over all contributing to the betterment and evolution of humanity and setting about true, right and natural lawfulness in the face of the misguidance's of the legal reality and its institutions and those who myopically and selfishly preserve and sustain them. Thank you to Frank O' Collins for their expertise in Roman Law, Santos Bonnaci for their presentations on the history of Unam Sanctum and the Cestui Que Trusts, the ever passionate Mark Stevens of the 'No State project.com' and Nathan Fraser in their ongoing campaigns in questioning government authority, the brilliantly articulate and informative Jerry Day of 'Freedom Taker.com', the ever insightful and straight forward Karl Lentz, the late John Harris of TPUC.org, the brave and brilliant Michael of Bernicia of 'thebernician.net' Scott Bartle another brave and brilliant human being of 'truth-now.net' for exposing this author to corporate governance, Rena Lliades maker of 'Pirates of the Suburbs' thank you for exposing also this dark corner of modern corporate/ governmental extortion, former activist and educator by the alias Thomas Anderson who peaked the curiosity of many with their talk 'The Strawman Illusion' and among those to rekindle interest in the subject in recent times, Veteran truther Max Igan of 'crowhouse.com', Frank van Dun Ph.D Dr.Jur for their excellent and clarifying essay 'Lawful and the legal', Retired Judge Anna von Reitz for their research and insight about the truths of the Birth Certificate, Murray Raff for their essay on globalisation of property law systems and torrens stewardship, 'wakeupwiki.com' for the excellently presented and compiled essay on global corporate governance: 'The New Zealand Government: A United States SEC Registered Corporation' among the many great legal and lawful source materials out there. To Peter Joseph, the Zeitgeist Movement and the many other NLRBE advocators active in helping the world realize what is not only possible but feasible. Final thanks goes to the late Jacque Fresco of the Venus Project whose life time of work and commitment have become an inspiration to many in realizing likewise, how the next step in our evolution can be made through a natural law resource-based economy, if not in part at least.

PREFACE

This work, to the knowledge of the author is perhaps the first attempt of its kind to bring together and bridge the subjects of the legal mechanisms controlling the world while suppressing the true and natural state of being that we should rightly live by in having the freedom of self determination while causing no harm or doing no wrongto another and that of the advocating of the economic paradigm of a Natural Law Resource -Based Economy (NLRBE) in order to live such a life.

Both camps indeed have their activists and educators, but again to the knowledge of this author have neither appeared to establish any real form of dialogue let alone awareness of the other in coming together in addressing the common problem: being that of the financial, economic and political frameworks of the world underlined by a legal system sustaining all three.

Those of the (NLRBE) camp are indeed aware of all three of these institutions and address them persistently of their faults, corruptions and detriments to the ongoing prosperity of both humanity and the planet, while those of the legal and lawful camp address equally well the faults, corruptions and detriments of the legal frame work while being aware of the entailing financial, economic and political institutions but appear to remain unaware of the opportunities let alone the feasibilities of a Natural Law Resource -Based Economy with some coming close to its philosophy with a global system of natural law and inherent land rights such as the present case with native and aboriginal situatons.

The bridging of the two is what this work directly intends to do in studying the what has been termed for the sake of this work *legal roadblocks* of the present *legal reality* which presently stand in the way of any possible transition to a Natural Law Resource -Based Economy, as the research and study efforts of this author detail and demonstrate in the following.

A final summarization is however offered as to how the legal reality may not be the barrier it appears to be and how certain aspects may in fact be a help more than a hindrance for the foreseeable future in establishing a Natural Law Resource -Based Economy. Before reading these conclusions the author strongly advises reading the book through and so understand the whole story having led to that point. An understanding won't be made unless what is read fully beforehand, indeed in knowing that past can ensure we know the future.

This work is hoped to be a timely springboard to further study to those both new and experienced in this subject matter. In coming to Learn and know the reality of both can further efforts for a truly free and prosperous world be made in thought, word and deed.

INTRODUCTION

There is what could rightly be dubbed a very real and detrimental *legal reality* pervading the world and likewise a very real and detrimental ignorance of how it works much like finance, controlling the lives of millions through such ignorance.

If those within the Natural Law Resource-Based Economy (NLRBE) advocating community and those otherwise are to help realise a planetary socioeconomic paradigm that has its resources both physically and intellectually fixed on social concern in balance with nature, as is currently not the case, instead being for the sake of economic growth and market prosperity, this reality indeed needs to be addressed and can be using the means and tools of scientific scrutiny and scepticism in compliment to the validity and place of the essence of man-made law known also as 'Natural Law' rightly enough.

The further purpose of the combined use of the two will be to objectively evaluate what benefits or detriments exist within this reality as regards to our social health as much as those concerning us of politics and finance, for in fact the very fabric of finance and politics throughout history always have had a legal underlining giving them longevity, power and influence of an evidently self-serving and preserving nature that time and again has proven to ultimately be a detriment to social health in the course of their operations while perpetuating a status quo of wealth and rule divide, and as a result the means for those in places of power, influence and wealth to exploit and control for their own self-preservation.

The following examples and sources are to help draw attention to and thus prove evidently the extent of this. Beginning with a general historical introduction to how this legal reality has come to dominate western society and the rest of the world through territorial jurisdictions and thus the peoples of the world who are made conduct themselves through forms of identification, taxation, licenses, fees, fines, permits, charges and so on. A brief but informative recap of the historical background of the origins of the western legal system is crucial so that relative aspects of the legal framework blanketing the earth can be comprehended fully in a modern context. From the Roman Empire and the Vatican to kings and monarchs to the foundation of parliaments and the what could rightly be called pseudo-democracy we have today of Presidents and Prime Ministers, how in reality governments of the majority across the world have either become or in part behave and operate as corporations due to fundamental changes made to the financial system in the early twentieth century and thus a major shift of the socioeconomic sphere itself, the result of which we are still dealing with to this day, often by-passing or even ignoring inalienable human rights and freedoms replacing them instead with privileges.

A QUICK ANALOGY

Although it may sound cliché by now to mention, considering the stage of social/ internet history we find ourselves in, of the now cult film *The Matrix* indeed no good truth-seeker or alternative news media website seems complete without a nod to this modern classic, does indeed deserve merit for giving the perfect analogy to this 'hidden-in-plain-sight' legal reality and are kept distracted from understanding and how it is part of the political and financial control apparatus slowly ticking away day by day feeding off of our life force and time to its clock and calendar, deciding our quality of life around its terms and conditions through its acts and statutes, making us use its fiat currency to survive while trying to convince us that material comfort and gain are the pinnacle of life here on earth through the use and control of mainstream media, advertising and the like, and that a living must be earned by the sweat of your brow; that nothing is for nothing, a scarcity and fear driven system indeed devoid of any scientific, intelligent or creative qualities which instead have come to subvert and control these for its own means of existence like the parasite that it is. This it will be seen plays into the heart of its aspects of operation but thankfully why there exist remedy in using scientific scrutiny to examine and critique coupled with lawful remedy and legal solution and no longer remain a roadblock indefinitely.

Those again of the NLRBE advocator community, or who otherwise wish to see a technical and scientifically sane world operating for social concern alongside environmental preservation and not that of market growth and efficiency for the benefit of the few, must first come to comprehend this legal framework of control and oppression being held in place and keeping things 'business as usual'. By studying its mode of operation, sceptically critiquing its history, theories, behaviours and actions; to ask the right questions so as no other conclusion can be made other than the fact it is essentially is an inhumane system incapable of providing what is required for the survival and prosperity of both humanity and the planet.

As J. Krishnamurti once said and as featured in the film of Zeitgeist Movement founder Peter Joseph *Zeitgeist Addendum* to simply -

> "Not accept things as they are... but to understand it, to go into it, to examine it, give your heart and your mind with everything that you have to find out a way of living differently - to understand is to transform what is."

The content explored in the following pages of the reality of how we are made interact with this Matrix may sound completely new and perhaps unbelievably shocking to some while familiar to others, so those who already know will understand the severity of the situation and how overcoming this 'road block ' will resolutely require a critical mass in numbers to ask in one voice by having these powers that be admit the truth; that the majority of the body politic are no more than chattel, slaves effectively with our time and energies only used solely to preserve the governmental, banking and other institutions of commerce and those atop the pyramid, be it the result of selfishness or fear and paranoia of losing control, believing there to be no other way, knowing what's best for humanity as if acting from some allegedly divine or higher law or position believing to be for the greater good, or perhaps simply not really knowng what to do but keep up the facade.

A work such as this encourages healthy questioning and criticism, such as why do we have to pay taxes if more money can be simply created every day and banks bailed out on a whim, why we need to give our signatures or a PIN number to access goods and services, why we need to be identified, monitored and regulated, fined and penalised, why we have birth and death certificates registered to begin with, isn't property registered? Why are we made to spend a lifetime paying fraudulent mortgages and loans to simply have a roof over our heads, even to exist. Who really owns the land anyway, government? Isn't government meant to represent the people, otherwise called a republic, democracy or commonwealth depending on where you are in the world and what country you were born in and a citizen or resident of?

In extreme circumstances of where they see fit government can force you off the land and if you try challenge them on it would be summoned to a court so far removed from constitutional or human rights as to be no longer relevant while leaving you bankrupt in lawyer fees. If you register children through the Birth Certificate or get a state marriage license government becomes a third party and can decide in such affairs, even take the child from you if they see a legal reason to do so, these what are essentially acts of violence on an innocent yet ignorant public are taking place constantly every day and all over the wolrd, make no mistake about it.

As this work will demonstrate, the institute of government has effectively become no more than a corporate entity in which to control and regulate our lives as no more than a glorified money collector and debtor to the banking system through taxation, fees and charges for the masses to have even a decent semblance of living such as owning and operating a vehicle and issuing of a tax file or social security number to have a job just to survive, as well as the multitude of invented taxes such as VAT. To again use an analogy from The Matrix movie, when the character Morpheus explained to Neo what humans in its dystopian future have merely become: a battery to power the machines with a creation and expiry date when all its life force is spent, is this to remain our fate?

DISCLAIMER

The following legal and lawful information and their historical accounts are not advised to be taken as professional or legal advice and are intended for educational purposes only. The views and opinions expressed by those featured are not that of the writers, having said, the information they base those views and opinions upon are obtanined largely or in part from established sources such as Canons of law as well as legal and financial practices and case studies which can also be used for one's own study and verification.

SECTION ONE
THE HISTORY

We will begin by examining some necessary historical socioeconomic background and key figures worth of mention in helping understand and establish the basis for the origins of legal involvement and place thereof in its history.

As a quick source of reference material The Zeitgeist Movement Defined will be used to give a brief but informative section on key socioeconomic figures and events before moving on to examples of legal association and significance from other sources, the authors of The Zeitgeist Movement Defined known to those within the movement among the audience of NLRBE advocators this essay is immediately intended for, have done fine work on researching and detailing the relevance of these figures and their theories in relation to the issue of market efficiency versus technical efficiency of both resource accumulation, distribution and consumption in relation to human labour input involvement in all three stages of this process at whatever stage of change or use of resources be it raw or goods conversion, as well as the debate on human consumption of resources and goods in relation to 'needs' and 'wants'.

The work as featured in *The Zeitgeist Movement Defined* help summarize two essential theories of economics and the free market: being Labour theory and Utility theory. Where Labour theory is the case of an owners versus worker relationship made to benefit the owners which could be viewed as realistic, whereas Utility theory attempts to remove this conflict of interests by seeing it as a relationship of mutual gain, being both too abstract and generalist in nature in trying to be a means to social harmony, removing any and all political and social aspects from the equation.

Such figures as French Economist Jean-Baptiste an exponent on Utility theory who tried taking into account the subjective rationalization of human decision making in the market as featured in *The Zeitgeist Movement Defined,* explained the contradictions of which pp - 77

"The exchange value (price) of any good or service depends entirely on its "use value" (utility) therefore this value equals its wealth. Although price is the measure of the value of things and their value the measure of their utility."

Being that individual pleasure is deemed the guiding and "moral " criteria of Utility theory leaves no realistic room for judgement, as subjective human input in regards to loss and gain, what is also referred to as "emotional dynamics" cannot be empirically calculated successfully either the variables being too great, which does however speak of a phenomena of the human condition within this circumstance, being that humans will and indeed do face the choice of either short term pain and loss for long term pleasure and satisfaction, or visa-versa, due to the prevailing socioeconomic conditions of the world perpetuated by political, legal and of course financial frameworks.

This is also otherwise referred to as 'Social Trap' being the tendency to pursue short-term gain in turn generating long-term losses being the case especially with resources when readily available and highly desirable resources and land for that matter, can cause people to compete for access and use and where long term costs are not visible or easily monitored.

The answer to this situation both past and present has been to invent laws as barriers to resources such as needing a fishing license and a catch quota. Effective social engineering as well as implementing laws would then be to reward cooperation with such laws and punish stealing and 'freeloading' to those who don't comply, the involvement then of economic forecasting to help increase visibility of long term costs completes this triumvirate of control. This one example could be extrapolated to many, many situations currently at play on a local and planetary level in regards to resource and land (as well as sea) management, where laws are invented as barriers yet always prove ineffective, such as that against poaching of endangered species, simply because there doesn't exist the man power or any real and effective scientific or technical solutions on a grand scale in which to tackle them, most commonly due to lack of funding or incentive. The same applies to the by now familiar case of transnational corporations devastating natural environments which until recent had no international legal platform to be challenged, a legal initiative spear headed by Ecuador under the U.N has been passed recently and now holds them more accountable for environmental degradation[1].

The Economist Nassau Senior postulated also the theory of human 'infinite wants' that humans will essentially always lack and remain unsatisfied of which material wealth could only gratify, as essentially hedonistic reflexes of fear of poverty and the behaviour of greed being part and parcel of human nature.

Retrospectively we can see the flaws of such theories if we pardon the time and socioeconomic conditions in which they were hypothesized much like other relative historical figures of Adam Smith, Ricardo, Malthus and Maynard Keanes of which none address in their theories the short comings of the market irrespective of their time periods coincidently, where essentially a belief is held that a 'free market' with free behaviour with a form of inherent and unspoken volunteerism will help maximize profits and gains for everyone through everyone's self-interest benefiting others with minimal

---

[1] Proposals for the New Legally Binding International Instrument on Transnational Corporations (TNCs) and Human Rights www.cetim.ch/8-proposals-for-the-new-legally-binding-international-instrument-on-transnational- corporations-tncs-and-human-rights-2/

government involvement. As explained in The Zeitgeist Movement Defined, pp.77 –

> "Nowhere in the writings of these thinkers, nor in the vast majority of works produced by later theorists in favour of free market capitalism, is the actual structure and process of production and distribution discussed. There is an explicit disconnect between "industry" and "business", with the former related to the technical/scientific process of true economic unfolding; with the latter only pertaining to the codified market dynamics and pursuit of profit."

Although this is true to a degree, studying this issue from a legal standpoint and the history revealed thereafter helps provide a different angle involving the otherwise nature of relationship existing between the populace, government, business and of course the banks, that economic theories and practice aside this legal framework has indeed had its own hand in shaping the evolutionary history of the global socioeconomic paradigm, most certainly in the west.

PROPERTY & OWNERSHIP
LAND, RESOURCES AND LABOUR

A suitable first example in the instance of any legal relevance to enter this study of the history of socioeconomics and figures of economic theory can be made with another reference from The Zeitgeist Movement Defined with the Economist Ricardo where stated, pp.72/73 –

> ' Ricardo's 1821 Principles of Political Economy and Taxation as quoted "The Product of the Earth at that is derived from its surface by the united application of labour, machinery and capital is divided among three classes of the community (1) the land proprietor (2) the capitalist (owner of the stock needed for its (the lands) cultivation (3) The labourers by whose industry it is cultivated. Tto determine the laws which regulate this distribution is the principle problem in political economy." '

In light of which it is safe to say not much has changed. This one paragraph alone provides all the evidence that is needed to justify the requirement of the study of a legal aspect in viewing the problems that stand before The Zeitgeist Movement, the greater NLRBE advocator community and all of humanity for that matter from achieving transition to an NLRBE.

If you were to guess of all the "classes of community" as Ricardo refers to it were the most important in this situation who do you think it would be? The answer being number one, the land proprietor, those with the right to ownership being a major point of study and as good a point as any to begin our understanding of the legal significance to the socioeconomic dilemma we find ourselves in. It is again crucial to study the history in helping gain understanding and context of how indeed not much has changed.

THE VATICAN AND THE HOLY SEE
A CASE STUDY

For the sake of a western context we'll begin with the example of the Vatican and to an extent the ancient Roman Empire. Some may be unawares to the relevance and influence of this ancient institution to social history outside of Religion, yet will become apparent for obvious reasons. Perhaps because no other institutions can rightly claim to be the oldest corporation on Earth nor have had the uniquely independent position to observe or become involved with the political landscape of Europe and the rest of the world at its own choosing from a position enjoyed only by monarchy as well as political and banking elites of the world.

It is hoped the audience know of the true reasons for the Crusades and Conquistadors from popular history and understand that Religion has always been central as a means to justify wars and profiteering, and where it is proven the Roman Catholic Church are guilty of their fair share. The Vatican has a long and colourful past being the subject of many books in itself. Perhaps the main reason for making it such a viable case study is by having done something unprecedented among all of the religions of the world, as some historians and researchers would verify by claiming ownership of the earth and everything on it and as will be seen has been at the heart of its purpose and agenda throughout its near two-thousand-year legacy in many ways. Researching the history of how the Vatican has obtained its vast riches, powers, influence, and land is a fascinating history of western culture in itself as to arguably be the oldest corporation in the world would indeed be foolish to pass over as a case study of its importance among what signifies a legal road block to an NLRBE.

FOUNDING THE HOLY CORPORATION

The Vatican began to grow in size and strength as the inheritor to the Western Roman Empire shortly after its fall. A major justification for the claims of the Vatican was that the Pope and thus all of the Church were the successors to Peter of the Apostles and thus God's earthly representatives and so the earth and all on it should fall under their claim of dominion and ownership doing so through legal means chiefly, religious indoctrination and practices secondly, and violence thirdly against heretics, pagans, barbarians and infidels through the use of crusades and inquisitions. The late Avro Manhattan (1914-1990) remains a leading independent expert on the Vatican and its history having written many fine and meticulous works, one of which 'The Vatican's Billions' details on p.19 –

> "The theory ran as follows: Christ is the lord of the whole world. At his departure he left his dominion to his representatives Peter and his successors. Therefore, the fullness of all spiritual and temporal power and dominion, the union of all rights and privileges, lies in the hands of the pope. Every Monarch, even the most powerful possesses only so much power and territory as the pope has transferred to him or finds good to allow him."

This in modern terms may seem outlandish and even laughable but aside from being a glimpse into a bygone age and how life and rule were conducted by an institution such as the Vatican, the same could be said of the divine right of Monarchs, the tyranny of dictators and of course the often corrupt practices today of pseudo democracies of Parliaments and Senates with their Prime Ministers and Presidents. For what indeed is giving them power, and why isn't it rebutted, a key word among legal terminology to keep in mind to be explored later.

As a momentary side tangent, constitutions of the west at least all have the notable commonality of being founded under God which has become a questionable concept in itself now more than ever and adds to the proof of just how antiquated the notion of government has become if not to self-evidently preserve the institution of elitism for the sake of land and resource ownership and control.

Continuing on with the Vatican, says Manhattan, p.12-

> "The establishment of the Papal States provided the Roman Catholic Church with a territorial and juridical base of paramount importance. From then on it enables her to launch upon the promotion of an ever bolder policy directed at the accelerated acquisition of additional lands, additional gold and additional status, prestige and power."

The origins of the Vatican obtaining its wealth and power concerns the submission of royalty and emperors of Europe and the British Isles to its Divine rule and with it all lands and riches through either this apparent right or legal means of which Avro Manhattan chronicles to be a history of deceit, forgery and fabrication. One such early example being the document the Vatican claim was given to them by the Emperor Constantine in 774 A.D. again detailed by Manhattan demonstrates the power inherited by this expressed Divine right, pp 12, 13 –

> "The significance and consequences of its appearance were portentous for the whole western world. The Social and Political framework of the Middle Ages were molded and shaped by its contents. With it the papacy, having made its boldest attempt at world dominion, succeeded in placing itself above the civil authorities of Europe, claiming to be the real possessor of lands ruled by Western potentates, and the supreme arbiter of the political life of all Christendom."

Furthermore, its clauses included -

> "Constantine desires to promote the Chair of Peter over the Empire and its seat on earth by bestowing on it imperial power and honour. The Chair of Peter shall have supreme authority over all churches of the world." "It shall be judge in all that concerns the service of God and the Christian. Faith."

16

As well such conditions such as -

> "The Roman clergy shall enjoy the high privileges of the Imperial Senate, being eligible to the dignity of patrician and having the right to wear decorations worn by the nobles under the Empire."

> "Constantine gives up the remaining sovereignty over Rome, the Provinces, cities and towns of the whole of Italy or of the Western Regions, to Pope Silvester and his successors."

The Church weren't happy there, building on their rights now by this 'Donation of Constantine' as has come to be known set out to claim dominion of all isles and lands as yet undiscovered. Again details Manhattan, p.20 -

> 'In the last clause of the donation: "Constantine gives up the remaining sovereignty over Rome..."and ending"...or of the western regions to Pope Sylvester and his successors" became foundation stones upon which the papacy demanded sovereignty, not only over practically the whole of Europe, but overall the islands of the oceans.'

This was achieved by the following means p.20 -

> "From then onwards by virtue of the Dominion of Constantine, the popes loudly claimed to be the feudal lords of all the islands of the ocean and started to dispose of them according to their will. Labouring to obtain papal supremacy, they used these rights as a powerful political bargaining power by which to further their political dominion over Europe: (a) by compelling kings to acknowledge them as their masters, (b) by granting to such Kings dominion over lands of which the papacy claimed ownership, and (c) by making the spiritual and political dominion of the Church supreme in the lands thus "let" to friendly nations."

LINES ON A MAP

As popular history tells us Christopher Columbus discovered Haiti and thus the Americas in 1492 as one of the first major expeditions of the age of discovery with other sea faring explorers from Spain, Portugal and Holland to follow, colonizing far away as South Africa, Oceania, Australia and New Zealand.

The Vatican were quick to claim the Americas first hand, for again by their Divine right all newly discovered lands and all the riches and treasures there within therefore belonged to the Pope and his successors. Some accounts given by Manhattan of this significant period demonstrate the Church at the height of its powers over Countries and their Monarchs include how in 1493 the Pope of the day granted Spain all the lands yet to be discovered on its conquests. A later Pope about this time granted the King of Portugal permission to possess all kingdoms and islands on its conquests also justified by of course being wrestled from 'the pagans and infidels'.

Just before the advent of the Protestant reformation the power and authority enjoyed by the Church began to wane, a number of figures began to speak out against the questionable 'Donation of Constantine' the bedrock of claim from which the Church had acquired so much wealth and power. However, this was not enough to slow the momentum of the Church which even by then in the 1500's had acquired so much land and riches and established so many palaces, churches, monasteries, nunneries and missionaries throughout Europe, the Americas and further afield that it could not be stopped. The situation of their wealth and power of influence became even more severe when in the year 1000 A.D. it was believed to be the end of the world and everyone from the lowliest peasant to the highest Monarch from all across Europe made the pilgrimage to Rome to be blessed for to enter heaven, even more wealthy donations filled the Church coffers across its territories in the form of gold, lands, estates and other valuables, legally of course.

Again details Manhattan by their cunning use of legal means in which to do so, p 26 -

> "The Church via her monastic orders and clergy, accepted the mounting offers of earthly riches. This she did by duly recording them with legal documents, witnesses and the like. To prove with matter-of-fact concreteness that the possessions of all those who had given were, from then on, the possessions of the papacy. It had been the most spectacular give away in history."

As well this event by the Church were others such in the year 1300 A.D when the Pope would pardon of their sins those who would make the pilgrimage to the Vatican for Christmas Eve and likewise accept donations from those who couldn't make the journey resulting again in vast donations of gold and other precious metals and on again for further events in the Church Calendar. Such events could be described as a swindle of giant proportions on an ignorant and gullible populace irrespective of class or status.

Further means were invented to extract more wealth on an ongoing basis which included using impassioned and tragically unbeknownst agents such as St. Bernard a proponent of practising poverty and hunter of heretics[2] who despite questioning the Vatican on its own love of wealth and riches only helped increase it by the fact of heretics having their property turned over to the Church if found guilty.

Says Manhattan of this. p27 -

> "St. Bernard had not been the first: he was one of many in a series of extirpators. But he gave a renewed impetus to the practice, since, with the increase of varied heresies and the even more varied -measures to suppress them, the very profitable method of

---

[2] Avro Manhattan – 'The Vatican's Billions' p.28 – The Corpus Juris, the Official law book of the Papacy, gave details: "The possessions of heretics are to be confiscated. In the Church's territories they are to go to the Church's treasury." This originally came from the last Emperor of Rome Justinian I who as Emperor had absolute control on Civil as well as Religious policy and thus granted the taking of the property of Heretics and turning it over to the Church and also granted monks the right to inherit property from private citizens and the right to receive 'solemnia' (annual gifts) from the Imperial treasury or from the taxes of certain provinces and he prohibited lay confiscation of monastic estates.

expropriating their property and levying crushing fines came increasingly to the fore."

The effect of the Church and its power and greed would long be felt in times to come; for its reach was long and actions merciless keeping in mind the extend of which having Monarchs at its bidding (Fig.1&2) such was written into the laws of the land; the Church essentially dictated by and large the rule of law and ruler of all it surveyed, riches and estates could be obtained merely by accusation of heresy, p 28 –

> "So it came to pass that the fulminations of the popes, for instance with launching anathemas, interdicts or excommunications in addition to arrest, torture and the death penalty, led also to the expropriation of all the goods, money and property of those who had been denounced."

Historical record can account for this lasting not years or decades but centuries, until there was a revolt within Christendom resulting in the Diet of Nuremburg of 1552 A.D. Always had the Church expressed their rule by the pen and not the sword, although could have said to do so with the Crusades indirectly. They essentially claimed to justify their actions and behaviours by Divine right which when unquestioned allowed for the creation and codification of even more laws which then became Canon such as the ploys of excommunication, being a heretic and having property ceased, as well as a right to donations and offer indulgences which in retrospect can clearly be seen as an organized and intended means to control, subvert and parasite off of the populace rich and poor like.

Fig.1 The Piano Nobile in the Vatican Apostolic palace gallery depicting the past donation of the kingdoms of Monarchs to the Holy Roman Church.

Fig.2 Mural of a Monarch donating their kingdom from the Piano Nobile in the Vatican Apostolic palace.

This by now may be sounding all too familiar to the powers and behaviours of the modern pseudo-democratic plutocracies of today and just why the Vatican and Roman Catholic Church make for such an excellent case study as the perfect theocratic comparison, where an institution can gain so much power and control when stand unrebutted ruling by fear, coercion, guilt and paranoia.

Another useful insight, again from Manhattan summarizes, p.31-

> "The Canonical tenants which the clergy invoked for their justifications were those implying that if an ancient custom is honourable and praiseworthy it acquires the binding force of law."

UNAM SANCTUM AND THE CESTUI QUE TRUSTS

Of all the history of the Roman Catholic Church, of its actions and practices none could said to be more notorious than what are known as the Cestui Que (pronounced setakay) Trusts issued through Papal Bulls, of which one would think the Vatican had gone truly mad with power.

Again the accounts given above date from just before 1000 A.D. till around the 1500s A.D. being exciting times for the Church and having its influence secured in history of the spreading of Catholicism along with land and riches acquired by the those who acted as their agents in the Monarchs and explorers who discovered and colonized the new lands in the name of Christendom. After this period the Church began to gradually loose its political and territorial hold of influence as the centuries passed[3] but its Canonical, legal and political influences still remain, as well as its arguably immense wealth it has managed to retain to the present day.

A number of researchers and historians have kept pace with the modern significance of the Vatican and of the notorious Cestui Que Trusts, for they demonstrate the boldest and one would say cunning arrogance of the Church by knowingly keeping the public in the dark as displayed by the Church at its political height in the Middle Ages. Essentially the Church declared its dominion over the earth and all on it by Divine right as stated, and the following is how it was done.

The Vatican and Popes between 1350-1550 A.D. enacted arguably the most controversial of their Papal Bulls the Cestui Que Trusts, but first declared the Papal Bull Unam Sanctum in 1302 A.D. which gave them rule over all kingdoms and monarchs of Europe[4] as a result of a response to a local

---

[3] Most notably with the Roman Question being a dispute regarding the temporal power of the popes as rulers of a civil territory in the context of the Italian Risorgimento: (unification of Italy into one kingdom) which ended with the Lateran Pacts between King Victor Emmanuel III of Italy and Pope Pius XI in 1929.

[4] This was to occur during the great Schism in the event of a division of Western Christendom into two camps with Pope Bonifice VIII issuing Unum Sanctum in 1302.
– 'The Atlas of the Bible and the History of Christianity pp.111.

political conflict with Philip IV, King of France involving the funding of a crusade as well as to express their authority over the rebellious king.

Unam Sanctum is still fiercely debated to this day, with Catholic apologists[5] saying it was only meant to refer to Catholics of its day notably the king, others would counter that claim by stating that nowhere in the bull is mentioned the name of King Philip or the nation of France, where it also states there is neither salvation nor the remission of sins outside of the Church, again no mention of just referring to Catholics and perhaps most significant of all, by leaning on the words of authority of the early church figure Saint Thomas Aquinas who stated that

> "it is absolutely necessary for salvation that every human creature be subject to the Roman Pontiff."[6]

Such grand and sweeping statements of divine and legal authority would indeed follow with the first Trust *Romanus Pontifex* issued in 1455 A.D. as permission for Portugal to claim all it discovered to the east as mentioned briefly before with the blessing and permission for King Alfonso of Portugal to conduct the following on sea faring discoveries –

> " We [therefore] weighing all and singular the premises with due meditation, and noting that since we had formerly by other letters of ours granted among other things free and ample faculty to the aforesaid King Alfonso -- to invade, search out, capture, vanquish, and subdue all Saracens and pagans whatsoever, and other enemies of Christ whosesoever placed, and the kingdoms, dukedoms, principalities, dominions, possessions, and all movable and immovable goods whatsoever held and possessed by them and to reduce their persons to perpetual slavery, and to apply and appropriate to himself and his successors the kingdoms, dukedoms, counties, principalities, dominions, possessions, and goods, and to convert them to his and their use and profit ."

As well-

---

[5] http://www.biblicalcatholic.com/apologetics/debate9.htm

[6] http://faculty.cua.edu/pennington/churchhistory220/LectureEight/UnamSanctam.htm

" That the same King Alfonso, his successors, and the infante, in the provinces, islands, and places already acquired, and to be acquired by him, may found and [cause to be] founded and built any churches, monasteries, or other pious places whatsoever; and also may send over to them any ecclesiastical persons whatsoever, as volunteers, both seculars, and regulars of any of the mendicant orders (with license, however, from their superiors), and that those persons may abide there as long as they shall live."

The second Trust *Aeterni Regis* issued in 1481 A.D was essentially a build on of *Romanus Pontifex* in terms of conquest and as mentioned in the quote below a further means to solve previous disputes of a treaty was it issued to resolve a dispute between Spain and Portugal again as an expression of divine and legal authority on the matter is stated therein -

" Of our own motion not in compliance with any petition offered to us on this subject, but of our spontaneous liberality, foresight, and certain knowledge, and from the plenitude of apostolic power, considering the letters of Nicholas and of Calixtus, our predecessors, the articles aforesaid [i.e The Treaty of Alcáçovas], as valid and acceptable, do by apostolic authority and tenor of these presents, approve and confirm them and everything contained in them and secure them by the protection of this present writing, decreeing that they, all and singular, ought to possess full authority and be <u>observed forever</u>. "

A further Bull *Inter Cetera* from May 3rd 1493 A.D was then granted to allow Spain to follow after Columbus and claim the Americas with the then Pope Alexander VI both literally and legally drawing a line of demarcation between the two poles, giving Spain the west and Portugal the east.

Finally, the *Trust Convocation* issued in 1531 A.D. which came into being as a result of a general assembly held by the Church in Trent as events were in crisis at the time with loss of territories, specifically demonstrates the supreme legal as well as ecclesiastical power the Vatican held over all of western Christendom, effectively commanding all they wished to attend to do so or face the wrath of the God, where stated -

"We summon, exhort and admonish, in whatever country they may be, all our venerable brethren, the patriarchs, archbishops, bishops, and our beloved sons, the abbots, as well as all others who by law or privilege have the right to sit in general councils and express their sentiments therein, enjoining and strictly commanding them by virtue of their oath to us and to this Holy See, and in virtue of holy obedience and under other penalties that by law or custom are usually imposed and proposed in the celebration of councils against absentees, that they attend and be present personally at this holy council, unless they should perchance be hindered by a just impediment, of which, however, they shall be obliged to give proof, in which case they must be represented by their lawful procurators and delegates."

This as well as the summoning of Emperors and Kings with what appears to be the main agenda of expelling the ongoing problem of infidels and barbarians from their territories, one can see the comparison between the Church's ploy and the 'War on Terror' today as an excuse to go to war and abuse diplomacy with aggressive foreign policies like that of the U.S, U.K and NATO in the Middle East.

If we study the history we see clearly the same patterns of control with Feudal lords, where protection from outside enemies being granted in return for working the land. Not much has changed really, as Peter Joseph founder of The Zeitgeist Movement has said on numerous occasions, we live in advanced feudalism, only the veils of apparent complexity and modernity again keep this hidden-in-plain-sight. Here we see the Vatican doing no different only using wrath of God to spread fear and guilt instead of modern government means of taxes, fines, fees and charges in order to secure and maintain its territories and the body politic therein with the use of legal mechanisms –

"And that this our letter and its contents may come to the knowledge of all whom it concerns, and that no one may plead ignorance as an excuse, particularly since there may not perchance be free access to all to whom it ought to be especially communicated, we wish and command that it be read publicly and in a loud voice by the messengers of our court or by some public notaries."

The mentioning here of public notaries is very significant and clue to the legal power of the Church inherited from the Roman Empire. The Church had evidently by this time developed a sophisticated enough administrative system and became responsible for the office of public notary with many clergy taking on the role throughout its territories. It was about this time from the late Renaissance through to the Middle Ages that Europe saw the modern development of the two main legal systems of the world being Civil law based on Roman law and Common law based on English law.

The Civil law notary to this day still remains a public official, the Common law counterpart to this role is a lawyer who has all the same duties and functions but can make court appearances also.

THE VATICAN AND ENGLISH MONARCHY

The history of the Church's power and influence over English Monarchy is a story in itself. As an interesting aside, in 1213 A.D the Pope positioned the Archbishop of Canterbury to be the Vatican's representative in England and to rule there under Canon law of which the then King John protested, with the penalty for doing so being his excommunication with later having to retract his protest so as to regain ecclesiastical and political favour with the Church. In that same year King John effectively gave control of England and all its territories to Pope Innocent III in the event known as the 'Concession of England to the Pope' where John swore in fealty by the Pope.[7] John later signed the Magna Carta in 1215 A.D to avoid rebellion from the Dukes, Lords and Nobles of the country but again had to renege on his actions and give his allegiance to the Papacy.[8]

Returning to the Convocation Trust, again asserting its full authority the Bull concludes on the following –

> "We command and decree also that an unshaken and firm faith be given to transcripts thereof, written or subscribed by the hand of a notary public and authenticated by the seal of some person constituted in ecclesiastical dignity.
>
> Therefore, let no one infringe this our letter of summons, announcement, convocation, statute, decree, command, precept and supplication, or with foolhardy boldness oppose it.
>
> But if anyone shall presume to attempt this, let him know that he will incur the indignation of Almighty God and of His Blessed Apostles Peter and Paul."

This document being replete with legalese upon closer examination is one resembling modern day martial law, in effect it is an order. Notaries were certainly appointed as one of the chief civic functions of the Church but the use of religious devices and the ever useful 'wrath of God' being

---

[7] A feudal tenant's or vassal's sworn loyalty to a lord.
[8] We return to this topic on pg125.

implemented as well. The Roman Imperial trait of an Emperor's word being law was carried on also for the Pope's remains the supreme authority of the Church being legislative, executive, and judicial.[9]

As the inheritors to the Roman Empire whose last bastion Justinian the 1st and his successors had created the foundations of western Civil law with the Justinianic Corpus Juris Civilis' (529-533 A.D) of which the Church amalgamated into its own Canon. Legal history shows that both modern Common and Civil law have influence of Ecclesiastical law as well, being after all the oldest system of law post-Roman Empire in the west, for after the fall and until the revival of Roman civil law in the 11th Century Ecclesiastical Canon law was the only functioning system in Europe. This system had its specialists and developed what the Church called the concept of 'a higher law of ultimate justice' about the time of the inquisitions as a sort of law above the law being the enforcing of a law pertaining to certain universal principles of fairness, morality and justice in an amalgamation of both Civil and Common jurisdictions. Modern day examples would be the Nuremburg trials of former staff of the Third Reich where even though argument was made they broke no laws under Hitler's regime an invoking of a higher law to seek justice for their crimes against other people, such as the Polish and Jews meant a higher law with respect to human life needed to be invoked to prosecute them, essentially more a case of morality than legality.[10]

The Convocation could be interpreted as written in this form by having a tone of perhaps tough love so to speak, to have all of these parties come together for a greater good and a greater purpose but certainly not for the two preceding it. The approving of and blessing of conquest through

---

[9] The Pope issues orders to the entire Roman Catholic Church and all under its Curia by what is called *Motu proprio*, Monarchs issue these also. It has its legal effect even if the reasons given for its issuance are found to be false or fraudulent, a fact which would normally render the document invalid. Its validity is based on its issuance by the pope by his own initiative, not upon the reasons alleged.

10 en.wikipedia.org /wiki/Rule_according_to_higher_law

slaughter and slavery is simply barbaric madness to modern ears, while the notion of being condemned for not being a Catholic and so the Church being in charge of you for your own good in the case of the Unum Sactum Bull, on the face of it again sounds utterly laughable and a pathetic assertion in the modern age, and yes it would be if not for Vatican's legal legacy having after all inherited and amalgamated the foundations of modern Civil law and thus playing a major role in shaping western civilisation while influencing English Common law and thus American Civil and Common law thereafter.

The Vatican having had plenty of time, experience and influence to become significantly recognized on the world stage, with the Pope still well regarded a figure of major influence and significance among western figureheads. The following examples however demonstrate the detrimental legacy it would help to create.

What of the lands, estates and riches the Vatican ceased over the centuries ?[11] Tracing and establishing original ownership of whether the Vatican have since returned or still hold title is as staggering to comprehend as to ascertain and beyond the capacity of this work and its author. However the events of the Vatican in the modern age as we will see however may help clarify this matter.

---

[11] https://www.theguardian.com/world/2013/jan/21/vatican-secret-property-empire-mussolini

THE NEW WORLD AND DOCTRINE OF DISCOVERY

Especially now with the outcomes of *Romanus Pontifex* and *Aeterni Regis* European countries and their rulers wanted in on the action such as the English expedition of 1583 to America with Sir Humphrey Gilbert being granted likewise power and approval to conquer unknown lands by Queen Elizabeth I (and through further blessing of the papacy). With such approvals new shores where sought out to conquest in Africa, Asia, Oceania and so on throughout the 16th and 17th centuries leading into the age of Imperialism and Colonialism and with it western legal systems of land ownership as well.

If we recall the Vatican's attitude to customs and laws[12] this attitude transgressed no less to Imperialism and Colonialism at the expense of Native nations particularly in the case of North America and Canada of this time due to what has become known as the 'Doctrine of Discovery' in the 18th Century having come on the backs of Columbus and the Conquistadors and their "God given" rights granted by these Papal bulls to, ultimately bring genocide and conquest in the name of Christendom and Commerce. Then, as stated by Steve Newcomb in their online article *Five Hundred Years of Injustice: The legacy of Fifteenth Century Religious Prejudice*[13] –

> "Over the next several centuries, these beliefs gave rise to the Doctrine of Discovery used by Spain, Portugal, England, France, and Holland - all Christian nations."

Newcomb then gives an account of how a Chief Justice John Marshall did the abominable by effectively writing the Doctrine of Discovery into the laws of the U.S.-

> "In 1823, the Christian Doctrine of Discovery was quietly adopted into U.S. law by the Supreme Court in the celebrated case,

---

[12] Avro Manhattan 'The Vaticans Billions', p30 - "The Canonical tenents which the clergy invoked for their justifications were those implying that if an ancient custom is honourable and praiseworthy it acquires the binding force of law.."

[13] ili.nativeweb.org /sdrm_art.html

Johnson v. McIntosh. Writing for a unanimous court, Chief Justice John Marshall observed that Christian European nations had assumed "ultimate dominion" over the lands of America during the Age of Discovery, and that - upon "discovery" - the Indians had lost "their rights to complete sovereignty, as independent nations," and only retained a right of "occupancy" in their lands. In other words, Indians nations were subject to the ultimate authority of the first nation of Christendom to claim possession of a given region of Indian lands."

He explains further from evidence obtained from a charter of an English Explorer of the time the validity and certainty of which -

"According to Marshall, the United States - upon winning its independence in 1776 - became a successor nation to the right of "discovery" and acquired the power of "dominion" from Great Britain. Of course, when Marshall first defined the principle of "discovery," when discussing legal precedent to support the court's findings, Marshall specifically cited the English charter issued to the explorer John Cabot, in order to document England's "complete recognition" of the Doctrine of Discovery. Then, paraphrasing the language of the charter, Marshall noted that Cabot was authorized to take possession of lands, "notwithstanding the occupancy of the natives, who were heathens, and, at the same time, admitting the prior title of any Christian people who may have made a previous discovery."

Newcomb then gives a further account of how this went onto apply to American Natives with a case of the Cherokee Nation -

"Using the principle of "discovery" as its premise, the Supreme Court stated in 1831 that the Cherokee Nation (and, by implication, all Indian nations) was not fully sovereign, but "may, perhaps," be deemed a "domestic dependent nation." [Cherokee Nation v. Georgia]

The federal government took this to mean that treaties made with Indian nations did not recognize Indian nations as free of U.S. control. According to the U.S. government, Indian nations were "domestic dependent nations" subject to the federal government's absolute legislative authority - known in law as "plenary power." Thus, the ancient doctrine of Christian discovery and its subjugation of "heathen" Indians were extended by the federal government into a mythical doctrine that the U.S. Constitution allows for governmental authority over Indian nations and their lands."

Examples of this plenary legislative power systematically drove Natives off of their Ancestral lands through the Indian Removal Act of 1835, the General Allotment Act of 1887 was then used as a ploy to take land from Natives and relocate them while avoid breaking previous solemn treaties the U.S. government made with Indian nations, thus systematically segregating them thereafter and the rest is yet another tragic and unjust account of world history and that of the U.S.

In conclusion of their article Newcomb states neither the plenary legislative power or Inter Cetera of 1493 have been revoked to this day, that the Doctrine of Discovery is essentially still in effect. The plenary power would be easier to have revoked being closer in the time of issuing while being contained within the jurisdiction of the U.S. Federal Government, and despite not citing specific examples of proof for the Inter Cetera an educated guess would have them mean it still exists through the Canonical/Civic systems in International law of which indeed the Vatican would be at the source of which in some major capacity, most surely. Despite any exact proof given one does not have to look far to find laws to the effect, having allowed the continued plunder and sale of the Americas, Africa, Asia and others by multinational corporations, through either the enforcement of policies from developed countries or the reception of developing ones through inept or corrupt leadership practices and lax labour and environmental laws.

THE CROWN AND CANADA

In Canada, the British Crown would have its own ploys to swindle and displace the Natives of their ancestral lands. In 1866 a Conference from Quebec went to London to have the Canadian Constitution drawn up only to be largely excluded from the process instead being done by just one U.K. Parliament Minister and Officers of the Colonial Office. What followed were a number of vague and unfair treaties with the Canadian Native Nations giving them privileges but no rights by agreeing. This however was technically a fraud to begin with as the Natives didn't speak English and therefore couldn't read to understand the terms and conditions of what they were agreeing to.

One notable figure, a teacher and politician Louis Riel who spoke both French and English was sought out by the Native people of Rupert land in Western Canada to help them from his reputation of trying to found a new province in Canada called Manitoba free of British Crown influence. A large part of the treaties was to move the Natives off of their ancestral lands and make them become farmers with promises of new equipment and livestock, which the Crown never followed through on. With poor equipment and not enough livestock to sustain them and their traditional way of life destroyed as well as no instruction on how to farm along with the spread of European settlers brought diseases such as small pox. The Natives began to suffer and starve to death when in 1885 the Northwest Rebellion broke out with Natives having to steal food and proper equipment from the European farms and forts to survive. The Army was brought into to capture and kill while many Native children were put in Catholic institutional homes only to face religious indoctrination, removal of natural identity and face sexual and physical abuses as they effectively became wards and property of the Crown Commonwealth of Canada under the conditions of agreed treaties. Louis Riel among eight Natives were captured and hung, not unlike heretics. The same patterns of abuse by both the British Crown and Roman Catholic Church have their histories elsewhere of which one can self-verify. The point of reiterating them here is not just for the sake of, but to bring awareness of how it was done; through inventions of legal manipulation and cunning to express their supposed authority first and foremost and to stand unchallenged of their claim of right and where necessary the use of physical violence in asserting it.

The odds were clearly stacked against the Natives of what might as well have been a rigged game, and indeed nothing has changed, as we will soon see and further proof why this legal reality the world has come to be dominated by cannot in anyway be a part of a NLRBE and must be taken seriously, as it is far too prone to contradiction, interpretation and above all corruption.

Least we forget this is all a system ultimately, and perhaps the most powerful ever devised, the pen is mightier than the sword and words even more so as they can control where and when that sword will be put and what the pen will write, and like all systems was made to a specific purpose with the examples given so far a testament of which.

THE VATICAN IN THE MODERN AGE

In the Introduction of their excellent book *The Vatican Empire* by the late investigative journalist Nino Le Bello, they stated-

> "The extent of papal wealth has been traditionally cloaked in secrecy. Even within the Vatican's own walls there is no one individual who has an overall view of its infinitely ramified financial operations."

Furthermore –

> "Vatican investment in real estate — one-third of Rome is owned by the Holy See — electronics, plastics, airlines, and chemical and engineering firms. - The Vatican is heavily involved in Italian banking and that it has huge deposits in foreign banks. Some of these accounts are in America, many are in Switzerland. The Vatican financiers prefer numbered Swiss accounts because they allow them to maintain anonymity when gaining control of foreign corporations."

A familiar pattern is recognizable, for instead of Monarchs, Barons, Nobles and Merchants being subservient to or in league with the Vatican we have Governments, Corporations, Entrepreneurs and Real Estate agents; makes no doubt the Vatican is both well familiar and practiced in keeping a foothold in the past and the other pointing to the future. So old is the Vatican and having acquired so much in near two millennia the combined value of the Vatican's wealth in Stocks, Bonds, Real Estate and Gold deposits and the total of Church Patrimony worldwide of Churches, Cathedrals, Monasteries, Nunneries as well as ancient buildings, antiques and artwork along with ancient manuscripts and other documents of historical value in its libraries and vaults, the sum of which would number easily in the billions.

The vault of catacombs known as the Vatican secret archives are said to run a number of miles in length (up to fifty) beneath it, spanning a history from the Eight century to the present day being first opened to outsiders in 1881, however materials from after 1939 are mainly off limits. Among its most famous documents are those relating to among others Renaissance figures Michelangelo and Galileo, Martin Luther of the Reformation and later figures such as Henry VIII and Abraham Lincoln.

The Vatican secret archives are arguably and speculatively an encyclopedic microcosm of recorded world history largely unknown to those outside of the church upper echelons, not seen or know of since the ancient library of Alexandria.

A Fortune magazine[14] article in 2014 on the Vatican's assets despite playing down its wealth as not even to make the fortune 500 still lists some pretty impressive figures with investments of a stocks, bonds and gold portfolio estimated at $920million USD, Real Estate holdings with an estimated worth of $1.35 billion USD and the Vatican Bank a book value of $972 million USD. It features also Church Patrimony particularly its art, antiques, artifacts and manuscripts which could easily fetch further millions if not billions but arguably priceless and in the Vatican's words 'belong to humanity'.

Again according to Nino's book The Vatican Empire the extrapolated wealth and influence of the Vatican in its modern form has been due to one man by the name of Bernardino Nogara. Being entrusted to administer a $90 Million inheritance granted from Mussonlini after the Lantern Treaty signed in 1929 Nogara would go on to use the amount in a worldwide investment policy. After his death in 1958 he left behind a methodology for his successors as the key to the Vatican's financial and business acumen while utilizing its worldwide tax exempt status and ambassadorial network in acquiring financial and business intelligence for stock market and shareholder investment decisions.

One of the key beliefs of Nogara was gold investment with the majority of the Vatican's deposits being held in the U.S. Federal Reserve. Nograra also established the practice of using Swiss and Federal Reserve accounts for business transactions and investments while avoiding Italian laws as well as keeping the Vatican's name out of the financial and mainstream media spotlight.

---

14 This pope means business http://fortune.com/2014/08/14/this-pope-means-business

Le Bello also detail throughout two chapters of their book the investment histories of the Vatican, though written in the 1960s gives a detailed account of the breath of activity at the time namely the construction company S.G.I (Societa Generale Immobiliare) later sold to former conglomerate Gulf and Western which had the Vatican as its biggest investor, constructed major real estate projects in and around Rome and other parts of Italy during the 1950s and 60s of residential units and hotels. Le Bello lists Vatican investment operations at the time to own major stakes in companies such as S.G.I and own considerable stake in smaller or partner companies who dealt with S.G.I so as to always have a steady income. Other construction projects within Italy included a major water dam project in Sardinia, the Milan underground metro, a major tunnel superhighway of Gran San Bernardo connecting Switzerland to Italy as well as numerous bridges throughout Italy.

They then detail the building of telecommunications and electric power plants and grids by companies with Vatican investment. Le Bello details also other now dissolved construction and real estate companies in the U.S. Mexico and Canada having had Vatican interests. One existing construction company 'Panedile Argentina' and long established Italian cement company 'Italcementi' have the Vatican as a major shareholder.

The Vatican also owns Italy's major gas provider 'Italgas' which in turn has controlling interests in a number of other companies in minerals, coke fuel and bottled water. It also has shares in a number of other energy and petrochemical Italian companies since the 1960s still in operation such as 'Novamount' and 'Edison' as well as India based aluminum company 'Madras Ltd' which is owned by 'Vedanta Resources' a global natural resources company dealing in Zinc, Lead, Silver, Copper, Iron Ore, Aluminium, Power and Oil & Gas. A recently insolvent producer of Chemicals and defense products 'SNIA' based in Milan also had large Vatican interests in its history. The Vatican also had its own textiles and ceramics companies but went insolvent in recent decades, no doubt due to shifts in the European and greater global geo-political and economic landscape of recent decades, and the competition of cheaper foreign imports.

Latest activities see the Vatican putting all efforts into its Museums as a consistent source of revenue while restructuring and reorganizing the Vatican bank to be more efficient, and transparent, as the secretive operations of the bank have resulted in scandal as the twentieth century dawned make it a wonder to many in banking, business and government how it has kept operations so opaque for so long in the modern age, the short answer being it have the legal means to do so namely being its own state and therefore having its own laws.

After the 1929 Stock market crash the Vatican played a major part in Italy's reinvigoration program the I.R.I 'Istituto di Ricostruzione Industriale.' (Institute for Industrial Reconstruction) which operated from 1933-1992 as a public law corporation of which the Italian government assigned specific entrepreneurial functions bringing vast complex of industries including television, radio, railroads, airlines, and shipping as well as steel, automobile manufacturing, and banking under government control but to operate and behave as like any free enterprise entity. It was a unique circumstance displaying the symbioses of the Italian and Vatican states. A historical election in 1948 also saw the Vatican throw its weight behind the Christian Democrat party to avert Communism taking hold in Italy, again a display of symbiotic and self-preservation in the name of free enterprise and the further involvement of the Christian Democrat party in the drafting of the Common Market Treaty forerunner to the EU, ironically of all perhaps being signed in Rome in 1957. Despite its dissolution in 1992 the party positioned the Church at the nexus of European politics in the twentieth century.

VATICAN PR

Another major issue in recent times for the Vatican being public image, over the last fifteen years of pedophilia scandals had the public being met with silence, the recent 'Vatileaks' concerning corruption and cronyism within the Vatican as well as promoting issues that have divided the Catholic community causing further insult to injury by not making any public apologies to any of the above instead being defensive, arrogant and aloof have cost the Church dearly with diminishing numbers among its clergy, the public attending church and most significantly diminishing donations and fund raising. As detailed in the Fortune Magazine article the Church is actually decentralized financially and administratively, the Vatican may manage its own finances and be answerable to no outside financial or government authority, of which the Vatican bank never published a public report on its books until recent[15] but the overall Church structure is split into three consisting of the Vatican, religious orders and dioceses and all independently responsible for their own finances, but still have to send annual donations back to the Vatican, old habits indeed die hard.

Interestingly the article in explaining this arrangement refers to each diocese as "a separate corporation with its own investments and budgets".

Having both money and public image problems pervade the Church despite having centuries of longevity understands it must adapt with the times or suffer the consequences of which both the twentieth and twenty first centuries are proving up to be perhaps in all its long and eventful history the most challenging due to competing and infringing socioeconomic factors. As for the Vatican itself, consequences would mean nothing dire in reality as its buildings and riches can't be confiscated by creditors or nationalized being

---

[15] Vatican moves to clean up finances money.cnn.com /2013/05/22/news/world/vatican-finances/index.html

its own state and only mean a change of tactic, of which they certainly have the ability.

Since the newest Pope Francis I took office, his humble image and public displays as the 'peoples pope' have done wonders with visitors to the Vatican trebelling since taking office, they know how to be PR Savvy. The Vatican's museums are among the fifth most visited in the world, having even gone so far to have rented out the Sistine Chapel in 2014 to a high end Charity Auction hosted by Car manufacturer's Porsche although the Vatican's press release stated it was not 'renting it out' but instead 'making it visible' for private groups, where the general public are given a window of just minutes to take in the grand Frescos of Michelangelo, attendees were wined and dined to a full concert on a 4,500 Euro a head ticket, call it what they will but money talks.

VATICAN BANKING

The Vatican bank has been in operation since the 1400s with connections and operations as old as the first merchant banks of Venice and the founding of the Bank of England, not much heed had been paid to it or even known about by the general public until the 1980s when a long serving Archbishop Paul C. Marcinku then head of the bank was involved in a scandal which centered around the collapse of Banco Ambrosiano, a bank in Milan with ties to the Vatican and Italy's largest investment bank of which the Vatican bank had shares. Missing money turned out to have been lent to 10 questionable companies controlled by the Vatican bank with a purported figure of up to one billion having gone missing. Vatican officials later agreed to pay $240 million to Ambrosiano's creditors but still deny any wrongdoing. Ambrosinano's president was a Mr. Roberto Calvi who was tried and convicted in connection with the scandal disappearing from Italy during his appeal and whose body was found hanging beneath a bridge in London in June of 1982. It was ruled a suicide but later homicide, while Marcinkus was indicted in 1982 in connection with the banking scandal. In 1987, the Italian constitutional court quashed the archbishop's arrest warrant as Vatican employees had diplomatic immunity from prosecution being outside its jurisdiction, while the Vatican also publicly denied any wrong doing by him or the bank.

This matter of Jurisdiction has also played into its sordid history. Being outside of Italian and EU jurisdiction the bank has had a reputation for money laundering and effectively being a tax haven having no mandate to deal with such things until 2011, as well as no Italian law requiring the bank to notify authorities of the identity of clients within Italy. Intended only for residents of the Vatican state this loophole soon had powerful Italian officials flocking to the Vatican to be granted accounts to avoid paying taxes. Before the adoption of the EURO Currency by Italy in 1999 the Vatican used the Italian Lira after which the Vatican has had to comply with EU monetary regulations and submit to auditing ever since. Recent steps also from both Pope Benedict XVI and the latest Pope Francis I to put an end to slush funds within the bank have seen 4000 accounts closed, a further step from Francis I has seen financial transparency relations between the Vatican and the EU improve by agreeing to follow policies on money laundering and financing of terrorism. One has to ask why now, again socioeconomic pressures of the twentieth and twenty first centuries are a strong clue, causing the Vatican and its hierarchy to act in contrary to the majority of its history, could the latest Pope genuinely be making the right decisions[16] to shake up the old guard for all the right reasons Is it possible to go against centuries of institutional self-interest and preservation.[17]

---

[16] Vatican 'may' consider divestment from fossil fuels, despite pope's call to arms
www.theguardian.com /environment/2015/jul/01/vatican-may-consider-divestment-from-fossil-fuels-despite- popes-call-to-arms

[17] The craziest financial schemes that the Vatican Bank tried to cover up
www.businessinsider.com.au /gods-bankers-financial-scandals-at-the-vatican-2015-2

GIVE UNTO CAESAR

The office of Pope is the last supreme emperor that exists in the world whose word is law over their Curia. These latest events may prove so far to be reforming the Church in certain areas while generating a positive image for it not seen since John Paul II, and who may be sincere in their actions, but certainly self and institutional preservation of the Vatican simply adapting to survive should not be ruled out, as there is too much at stake. The Church suddenly isn't going to step away from politics and the levity of influence having spend centuries establishing, nor renounce financial holdings as well as stocks and shares among the many banks and corporations having spent decades cultivating or reorganize its orders and dioceses to suddenly cease operations, as far too many livelihoods depend on it and that far too many have faith in, as well as of course to keep donations rolling in.

The Vatican and to that extent all that it encompasses is a law unto itself, much like a Monarch it is sovereign, while being proof of the myth that Church and State are separate, for they have not and never have been in the west, certainly in the legal sense.

A MODEL EXAMPLE

It is hoped the above information and references have sufficiently proven the Vatican to be arguably the most definite and archetypical institute of its kind for all else to follow in the history of western government, banking and business.

Being the oldest institution of its kind following the days of classical empire with partial success also being attributed to its ability to adapt to the changes facing it, one could say by and large wrote the book on the legal structures of modern western governance having inherited one of the most enduring of legal systems created with Roman Civil law, much like Emperor Constantine amalgamating Christianity with paganism, so too have his forbearers amalgamate civil and ecclesiastical canons in the development of corporate strategy and mandate by way of legal and ecclesiastical instrument upon acquiring vast wealth of land and riches as well as considerable political influence. All the while having a hand in perpetuating the corrupt and fraudulent nature and practices of banking and tax havens.

As well as the Holy Roman Church and Roman Empire that preceded it other notable detrimetal practices and institutions would eventually come to the west and the rest of the world there eafter effectively over time in the form of historically Jewish legal and monetary backgrounds. Key events in history of which will be examined in later chapters.

Le Bello in closing their book reiterate a speech given by Pope Paul in 1967 in his *'Encyclical Populorum Progressio'* (On the Development of Peoples) foreseeing the destructiveness of liberal capitalism that has since taken hold, despite condemning its fallacies said nothing of the Church to cease any involvement. Even with the latest Pope Francis I paying such lip service to preach of the evils of abusive banking and liberal capitalism has shown nothing beyond banking reforms and the vain attempt to bring abuses within the Church to task in issuing their 2013 Apostolic letter.[18] Self-preservation rules the day.

Above all the Vatican has proven and maintained that the pen is indeed mightier than the sword and that paper is more to be feared than standing armies. Through the issuing of contracts and trusts in its papal bulls throughout the centuries holding accountable friend and foe alike, all the while having made full use of the power of faith, belief and divinity to claim its right of power and position over the body politic and the earth on which it stands as it had in the past, now and for the future in whatever form ensures its survival, be it ecclesiastical, legal or financial. Western government and rule having followed suit, couldn't have asked for a better role model.

---

[18] http://w2.vatican.va/content/francesco/en/motu_proprio/documents/papa-francesco-motu-proprio_20130711_organi-giudiziari.html

THE LEGAL COMMONALITY

It is no secret that governments have become more and more publically brazen in their cooperation and submission to the demands of the corporate and the banking powers of which there is a history to prove, as bailing out of banks is really noting new and the consolidation of resources, money and power into the hands of the few seem unending.

The latest events of the TTP, TTIP and TISA[19] if given the green light are set to play out like a plutocracy wet dream, which will essentially grant Corporations the right to reinvent themselves into their own sovereign states, having their own closed law courts, diplomatic immunities and tax-free status, but perhaps is a way for the world political powers to deter off shore banking and the allure of tax havens to their corporate and banking counterparts, will however mean them having the same rights and powers as governments. As briefly mentioned at the beginning of this work for those unawares, the institution of true de jure government itself has long been corporatized in becoming de facto in nature in the west and increasingly throughout the world. Already such public demonstrations only prove how the lines are being blurred, and how all will eventually be consolidated under the banner of commerce with constitutions and human rights charters as mere window dressing as really only a soft sell; a farce given to the body politic so as to keep them away from the truth of the matter and how the world truly operates.

As long as there exists a legal paradigm to maintain them there will always be Popes, Monarchs, Presidents, Prime ministers and Politicians, and yet much like any other corporate or government entity within this

---

19 WikiLeaks - The US strategy to create a new global legal and economic system: TPP, TTIP, TISA. https://www.youtube.com/watch?v=Rw7P0RGZQxQ

socioeconomic system having proven themselves to be none different and indeed never have been. For government, corporations, banks and even Churches all have the same commonality of being established and operating from the same legal standpoint, while having the public coercively, and as with the majority unwittingly become subservient to them by not questioning this apparent and self-elected power and authority through legal manipulation and control.

THE LEGAL REALITY

Knowing how important an issue the researching and verifying of this legal reality is to the future prosperity of humanity while attempting to bring a convincing enough argument to the NLRBE advocator community and those otherwise of its seriousness, as much as that already understood of the detriments of Capitalism and the Monetary system, proves no easy task. Having the input of knowledgeable individuals, verifiable and acknowledged sources of reference along with breaking events and trends help greatly in piecing it all together.

A fitting analogy comes to mind for the body of information ahead from one of the authors favorite artistic figures which can indeed be applied to any area of life, comes from the French Impressionist painter Pissarro when asked once how they approach a painting said simply 'start with the broom and end with the needle!'

The previous case study of the Vatican and the general study of government, banking and commerce structures have helped shed light on a number of factors and their authority:

- It is assumed and stands as thus when without rebuttal, while being met with silence or proof of claim.

- The Body Politic will always be convinced there is a reason for authority to exist and that they will always need it, but must pay a price for the privilege.

- We must accept this authority by giving our consent to it and are made do so through many means (Participate, consent, permission, submit, acknowledge, agree, understand.)

This is further solidified by the legal reality framework and its methods in getting the public to consent, this is the starting point without which force must be used such as martial law, actually we just have to look at the language used as proof that there is hardly such a thing as consensual government, for when a statute or act is brought into effect it is done so with force; through the force of law. These are among the means to be found everywhere in society to be examined in this section such as contract, from simply opening mail to buying a pack of gum are all essentially offer and acceptance, however with Statutes the system has been designed deliberately so as to coerce you into acceptance by silence or to respond with conditional acceptance. In some case's a conditional acceptance may not even be allowed even though a statute is rightly given the force of law through consent of the governed of which even the majority of the general public remain unawares to.

However not only do the law makers and practitioners know this but can and indeed do try 'shift the goal posts' when challenged, hence the amalgamation of legal systems and the blurriness of what jurisprudence and legal sub-sections a case may fall under such as with English and American Common law becoming amalgamated with Statutory law while being predicated on case law where a Judge may decide the outcome of a case often irrespective of the facts, essentially being a law unto themselves. Judges at district level will even go so far as to deny a Supreme court ruling as they are often the barrier to justice in favour of the establishment and banks.[20]

---

[20] As will be demonstrated regarding a case study concerning mortgage law later.

KNOWING THE REALITY

The legal reality has deliberately been created to appear highly confusing and complex. This work is an earnest attempt to cover some of the most important and fundamentally relevant aspects while avoiding any confusing and unnecessary topics or jargon.

There is good reason why law professionals exist of which this author makes no claims to be, but as with any subject or area in life there is a certain degree of information accessible to the layman, and being of the fact that we don't want to entertain more than we need to know of this system while using our common sense and better judgment in asking the right questions to the right people, can we expose this global fraud and succeed, for we will be in the right while acting honorably in bringing about the truth of the matter while having the advantage of the outsiders perspective.

Having said, there are ongoing efforts of ordinary people trying to challenge the legal system to become free of it. There exists also an online culture of what has become called Freeman, lawful rebellion, legal remedy and commercial redemption movements (just to give them names, as not all those involved necessarily fit such terms as we will come to examine and try understand in the third and last section of this work.)

A classic example of this abuse by government and corporations is in the case of utilities[21] where a large number of examples may be found of either being made private, raising prices and/or providing less than adequate service so as public backlash ensues, causing pressure to then typically follow from the public for government to fix the situation, to either

---

21 Privatization of Water as an Owned Commodity Rather Than a Universal Human Right
http://www.globalresearch.ca/privatization-of-water-as-an-owned-commodity-rather-than-a-universal-human-right/5378483

have the private company follow a standard to improve services or have government buy back the utility and make it public once again, and so we have the legal framework doing as it should; to work for the people not exploit or suppress them, but again as with all things in 'legal-land' the seemingly impossible can often be made possible with the invention of semi-state bodies, followed by more impasse and bureaucratic processes where the issue is proverbially kicked down the road, typically until a next election. Kicking things down the road in anything socio-economically related appears to be the order of the day with governments no matter the country, and being the basis of the world financial system ever since the 1930s as there has been no real money in circulation since only borrowed credit backed by future revenue generated from the labour of the masses, GNP and GDP to pay back national debt owed to the banks exists as well as speculative trading of currencies, the world runs essentially on promises to pay.

Earlier postulations judging from recent behaviours of the Vatican being perhaps due to rapid increases in scientific, technological and cultural progresses of the modern age, could likewise be applied to government and so with commerce and banking. It seems the powers that be need to keep society in the past and adhered to established and absolute concepts in conducting society at large, perhaps then explaining the phenomena of science and technology racing ahead while the socioeconomic structure remain deliberately stagnated.

Again from *The Zeitgeist Movement Defined* in the section: *The Final Argument: Human Nature* offers the following relevant insight -

> "The overall basis of the market concept has to do fundamentally with assumptions related to human behavior, traditional values and an intuitive view of history- not emergent reasoning, actual health measures, technical or ecological responsibility."

Is this what the establishment perhaps are afraid of, that we need minders, that we aren't capable of self-responsibility and where a higher law need be in place for our own good, indeed the greater good. Needless to say the nanny state is in full swing coupled with a post Orwellian surveillance apparatus in overdrive [22] constantly monitoring our behaviors for feedback then used to cultivate and adapt this archaic authoritative and commercial framework for its benefactors while keeping us constantly engaged and distracted with it of which the public are now fully aware of in thanks most notably to the efforts and sacrifices of Edward Snowden, Chelsea Manning and Julian Assange with Wikileaks among others.

The political philosopher Thomas Hobbes once argued that life would be brutal and violent without political law and order, where people having the right to do anything would only end up raping, pillaging and plundering in chaos and violence. He saw the solution in allowing people to socially contract freely to establish a civil society, however believing also that there must be a monarchy to be subjective to and maintain over all order. We see plenty of cases of modern day riots and those among The Zeitgeist Movement and others similar know all too well why they continue to occur, being due to a fundamentally outdated socioeconomic structure that while indeed has human behavior at its heart is fundamentally due to the influence of environmental conditions, and so the vicious cycle continues.

The aspect however of Hobbes statement to socially contract freely is very much in tune with the Natural law paradigm and could well be part of a means of transition to a NLRBE. On the surface one may think from observing the "free market" that people and whole businesses already trade with one another freely, but little understand that they do so while having to pay taxes, register their business, obtain licenses and permits and submit to health and safety regulations with government always having its hand in their pocket.

This is part of what being free to contract in Natural law means: by no government interference, to honour one's contracts while doing no harm. The dominant legal reality has resulted in an overly complicated

---

[22] New Study Shows Mass Surveillance Breeds Meekness, Fear and Self-Censorship theintercept.com /2016/04/28/new-study-shows-mass-surveillance-breeds-meekness-fear-and-self- censorship/

socioeconomic system for obvious reasons, so as to generate revenue in all aspects of living while removing personal accountability in hiding behind corporate and legal entities with the requirement insurances and to sue for loses.

THE LAWFUL AND THE LEGAL
A WORLD OF DIFFERENCE

As stated from the beginning of this work, the masses generally are ignorant to the influence of the legal as well as financial mechanisms dictating their lives. Here now we can begin to examine and understand the details of that reality, how it works and by what means. A good place to begin is with the origins of the language of this legal construct, for as may generally be known, the legal profession or otherwise called 'law society' has its own language of legalese, as a quick comparison to the monetary system having its own language of terms and descriptions used by professionals the general public have been kept ignorant of while being led to believe they couldn't possibly comprehend and just why legal and financial experts are required.

What is legal and lawful will come to be understood are often complete opposites. It is a sad Irony that the legal system is generally known as 'law' 'law school' 'law society' and so on, but is totally unlawful, the true meaning of the term has been hijacked in both a socially and commercially applied sense as Prof. Frank van Dun a senior lecturer in the Philosophy of Law states in their excellent Essay *'The Lawful and the Legal'* -

'The "education in law" these schools provide resembles nothing so much as an initiation in the rites and customs of a particular profession, its dogmas, doctrines and prejudices, especially concerning the so-called "sources of law": legislative, judicial and administrative rulings, treaties and the main currents of opinion among the members of the profession. Positivism has rationalized the idea that "law" has its sources in the decisions of designated political and professional authorities.

Saying further-

> "By equating the lawful and the legal, it has helped to push the study and practice of law away from considerations of justice into a mere expertise in legality."

This Essay by van Dun will be used as a chief reference throughout this section for its demonstration of the origins of many words which form the basis of both legal and lawful lexicon as featured to be of Latin, French, German, Dutch and English origin among them being definitions of Right, Justice, Citizen and Freedom. Before this however, some introductory material on the difference in definition and application of the two is useful.

NATURAL AND COMMON LAW

Societies all across the world down through the ages from the tribe to the village to towns and eventually cities have always had some form of resolving matters and disputes for wrong doing perhaps over some material goods, or even such things as adultery. These were never originally written down but passed orally to be kept and upheld, this came to form the basis of Natural law; inalienable and universal, being essentially a system of peace keeping, respect and conviviality among peoples within families and the greater community regardless of social status or rank.

The system works by dispute and resolution being local as within a tribe, band, or community. Judges are traditionally respected community members. A court would consist of a group of community members coming together to assist in resolving a dispute. Members of the court are selected and agreed upon by both parties in the dispute. The members also volunteer only for the duration of a case. As we well know we are moving into a future that if managed and cultivated correctly as proposed in a NLRBE that such requirements for dispute resolution would become a thing of the past, while there's nothing inherently wrong with this system as it solves a problem peacefully and cooperatively where both parties can reach an agreement is already done so everyday around the world in everyday life between people themselves. In their Essay van Dun explains of Natural law in essence –

> "Natural law theory properly understood is not some sort of normative moral theory. It does not seek to make moral judgements. It seeks to identify the principles of social order, to judge human actions as either lawful or unlawful, depending on their relation to such actions."

Where also saying –

> "In short, Natural law is made to appear as an ideal legal system, with the distinguishing characteristic that its validity. Natural law has become looked down upon as too simplistic"

Natural Law has over time fallen into obscurity with academic curricula of law and is regarded to be no more than a philosophical relic, as no longer fitting the needs of commerce though it can't ignore having some of its origins from them. Simply being, that as society became more complex and with it more commercialized Positive law equally became so too alongside, governments and corporations became more complex and thus more compartmentalized, specialized and bureaucratic where today governments create more and more acts and statutes annually for policies than anytime previous to the twentieth century.

It has found a resurgence in recent decades among movements of ordinary people around the world becoming educated on its origins and use for a number of cases thanks to the internet, where their natural rights are being taken away or infringed upon as a way to find peaceful and lawful solutions in what has become known as 'lawful rebellion' a story in itself that will be covered a bit later.

Common law in essence is an extension of Natural law; where Natural law represents peace, respect and conviviality among all members within a community Common law carries these principles forward into conducting relationships with others in more complex environs and situations while sharing a well-known axiom 'one's freedom ends where another begins'. In

Common law a crime is one with a victim, an actual human being who has been stolen from, physically assaulted or murdered.

The English and American Common law systems still retain the essence of Natural law as with murder trials and due process with a grand jury's decision being final and standing as law. Another interesting point of contrast being that in Natural law jurisdiction is whatever the parties in dispute decide upon, whereas English Common law jurisdiction includes any government transgressions such as breaking of articles of security or peace or anyone having being abused by government. Modern juries agree to prescribed written laws on natural justice such as the Magna Carta or Bill of Rights.

The English Common law system established the modern court system as prevalent today. It deals also in private law of that which governs relationships between individuals including Law of Contracts, Law of Torts, and Civil Law (labor law, commercial law, corporate law). It is also based on precedent being the prior decisions of formal courts and judges. It is also hierarchical with judges deemed authority figures. Lower courts are subject to higher court decisions. State or federal judges often also rule on cases from outside their own community.

CIVIL AND COMMERCIAL LAW

An online article *Natural law, Positive law* [23] gives a definitive description to the modern guise of Civil and Commercial law, the core of the legal reality –

> "Law', indeed, now usually refers to some national system of social regulation – a system of social regulation <u>imposed</u> by the rulers of a nation-state and otherwise coordinated by their agents and servants. By extension, 'law' now refers also to regulatory systems to which the rulers and diplomatic agents of various nation-states have agreed.

What follows from this same article is crucially important and really gets to the crux of the matter of just why the power structures want Natural law banished to the history books. Emphasis to the last sentence has been added to highlight the important points that are to follow, of the nature of relationship that has been deliberately created between humanity and the power structures of Government, Banking and Commerce, of how humanity have in fact come to be seen as merely Chattel and all proof of our natural and inalienable rights be erased –

> "All of this goes under the academic label of 'positive law', which covers any one of the many particular imposed ('posited') systems of regulation by legal rules that we find in various politically organized societies in its legislative, executive, administrative, judiciary and military and police 'organs', its offices and officers, the rules they follow and apply, and the decisions they make. **Those systems have no necessary connection with natural law or justice. They define only what is legal in a particular society, not what is lawful among human beings."**

---

[23] users.ugent.be/~frvandun/Texts/Logica/NaturalLaw.htm

WHEN IN ROME

The old familiar saying all roads lead to Rome has even more levity perhaps when considered from a legal perspective. The Roman Empire built vast networks of roads throughout its territories along already popular trade routes and charged a toll to use them. Considering how the modern legal reality has Roman origins explains why modern commerce still operates on such premise, leaving no choice for the body politic but to use its system or face the consequences.

Those enforcing it may have changed guise yet the system and ideas remains, making Civil based 'Commercial' law effectively the dominant system of law in the world overlaying Common law while constantly being updated to fit the needs of the machinery of Capitalism and Globalization, the new empire, for the powers that be understand its effectiveness and why there has been a constant push to consolidate the world into trade partnerships and territories, bringing more and more countries under its jurisdiction such as with the WTO and the GATT agreement, The north and south American CAFTA, NAFTA agreements as well as the EU and its treaties, and now with the TTIP and TPP agreements all coming from the same empirical model only to be more complex and extrapolated for a modern world.

As to demonstrate such historical origins a useful passage from a work titled Historical Jurisprudence by Guy Carlton Lee of Johns Hopkins University in 1922 is worth quoting –

> "Modern "Commercial Law" Is based on Ancient Babylonian Codes the source of English & American Civil Law. Civil Law is recognized in Black's Law Dictionary as synonymous with "Municipal Law". Rome is well recognizable as an Aggressively Warring & Conquering nation. Textbooks say that the conquered cities "were compelled to pay the war-tax" ... "a town thus treated was known as a municipum or "burden-holder"." Many of the conquered peoples were reduced to Slaves. The Roman merchants engaged in much Slave Trade. They established Slave-

markets. Contracts exchanged hands among merchants for the delivery of Slaves. The Codes which governed these contracts for Slaves were based on the same Codes which the Babylonians had developed. "Of ... these Rome was ...possessed from the earliest period ..."

OLD HISTORY, MODERN CONSEQUENCES

One of the main aims of this work is to highlight how despite being however old a system of law in essence or in practice still can have modern significance by simply becoming updated and codified over time under new definitions and titles. If there is one sure constant regarding law and government being when it comes to Acts and Statutes are easy to create but hard to abolish.

A good example helping prove this features in an article Modern "Commercial Law" Is based on Ancient Babylonian Codes concerning the events of the 11th century Norman Invasion of England which led to the infiltration of the ancient system of English Common law and land ownership system setting the course of history to the detriment of western civilization for generations to come with these laws being retained in the British legal system and spread out over the world as part of its Commonwealth Empire which still applies to this very day. A reiteration of events is given as follows -

> "The Norman (French) Conquest over the Anglo-Saxon/Celtic people of England in 1066 is vastly underrated in its significance to understanding modern considerations of good government. From Rome, it had the "Solemn Blessings of the Pope". The Pharisaical system of "Babylonian Talmudian" based "Commercial Law" was at that time Forcibly Imposed over the Christian-Common Law English People."

Explaining further (emphasis added) -

> "Several elements of historical (Jewish legal practice have been integrated into the English legal system. Notable among these is the written credit agreement - shetar, or Starr, as it appears in English documents. **The basis of the shetar, or "Jewish Gage," was a lien on all property (including realty) that has been traced as a source of the modern mortgage.** Under Jewish law, the shetar permitted a creditor to proceed against all the goods and land of the defaulting debtor. ... Jewish law that debts could be recovered against a loan secured by **"all property, movable and immovable" was a weapon of socio-economic change that tore the fabric of**

feudal society and established the power of liquid wealth in place of land holding."

This led further onto the establishing of equity courts of which the Vatican further gave the Norman conquest its blessing thus establishing it under Roman Civil/Municipal Codes.

"These courts were the essence of the so-called Equity Jurisdiction. It was all run by Chancery Priests, & referred to in deceptively as "Courts of Equity", the only thing being "Equal" about them is that all Conquered "Slaves" there under are treated more or less Equally. "Courts of Chancery" is a more honest name, as it was great "Chance" taken to go before such."

Also detailed are the historical implications of which in leading to the foundation of modern western legal systems, where citing Bovier's Law Dictionary of 1868 namely that of the U.K. and U.S.-

"The whole of equity jurisprudence prevailing in England & the United States is mainly based on the civil law" - "Civil Law" is from Rome. There was no "Equity Jurisprudence" in England prior to the Norman Conquest'.

THE WORLD'S LEGAL SYSTEMS

Another piece titled 'English Common Law is now the most widespread legal system in the world' from an article by legal and professional information providers Sweet & Maxwell and Thomas Reuters featuring the research of Professor Philip Wood, Special Global Counsel at a leading international law firm Allen & Overy having been the first person ever to undertake a truly comprehensive study of how the world is governed by legal systems. In their findings the top three systems were English Common law, Napoleonic law and American Common law. Of this fact they detail -

> "English Common Law is the most common legal system in the world, not only because it applies to the largest slice of the world's population but also because it is used in 27% of the 320 world's legal jurisdictions."

Further saying of the others -

> "Napoleonic Law, which is used in countries such as Brazil as well as France, applies to the largest share of the world's land mass (34%). It is originally based on the codification of French law under Napoleon and covers 23% of the world's population. Napoleonic Law jurisdictions represent 23% of the world's GDP."
> - Napoleonic law was spread by the French Empire and by emulation. Egypt is one example of a country that kept Napoleonic law after it was occupied by the French in the Napoleonic Wars - Some countries, particularly in Latin America, adopted Napoleonic law because the code was the most advanced contemporary model to borrow from at the time that they were looking to formalize a legal system." - "Although the American Common Law group only covers 5% of the world's population in terms of legal control, Philip Wood shows that the American Common Law jurisdictions' GDP accounts for 26% of the world total. Outside of the US American Common Law has been adopted by a limited number of countries such as Liberia and unincorporated US territories such as Guam and Puerto Rico."

As well as mapping these jurisdictions and the percentage in population who live under them the recording of monetary activities likewise was undertaken. Says Professor Wood of his findings with the English and American Jurisdictions –

> "In examining the various legal jurisdictions, Philip Wood shows that the defining characteristics between the jurisdictions are their attitudes to debt, credit and insolvency. American and English Common Law generally favours the creditor in insolvency issues, while Napoleonic systems tend to favour the debtor."

Stating further -

> "The combined share or GDP of 40% for English and American Common Law demonstrates how much influence their treatment of debt and attitude to creditors has over how the global markets operate."

Anyone who has paid attention to the history of western commercial, banking and governmental behavior models in the treatment of debtors will be none too surprised with the validity of such evidence and further proof of the power of legal instrument as much if not more than that of the monetary system or free market orientated economics, for without the legal means they would not exist nor function as they do so.

Although political and legal systems have never appeared to evolve as fast a pace as science and technology, has perhaps been a different and deliberate kind of evolution as we can clearly see from their lasting impact. Noting besides stone monuments arguably say more about a civilization that its system of jurisprudence. [24] From Ancient Babylon and Rome to the legacy of the Vatican, the enduring U.K. Commonwealth and modern U.S Empire are the story of a legal reality thousands of years in the making essentially accumulating in the story of commerce.

---

24 See world map of legal systems on at
https://commons.wikimedia.org/wiki/File:Map_of_the_Legal_systems_of_the_world_(en).png

Yet, it is a system that many of us can see to have outgrown its usefulness, with its place and purpose evidently showing time and again as being only to preserve the wealth gap and class divide across the world for the self-preservation of the political, financial and business institutions and classes.

TRUTHS ABOUT CONSTITUTION AND CITIZENSHIP

Being that civilization is shaped by factors of environmental, having a system of jurisprudence and therefore a language in which to exercise such a system likewise can affect it significantly.

In understanding the origins of words and their application in this Legal Reality framework can we know our place in it, where again the work of Prof. van Dun with their Essay *The lawful and the legal* demonstrate a number of key words and definitions in helping understand and clarify what it is to have legal and lawful standing between ourselves, government and commercial powers, indeed a very important point of topic in reasons why the body politic are made to pay taxes among numerous other impositions government will try and have them comply with or face penalties, to consider the following –

> "At the risk of confusing equal justice with equal treatment, equal justice is achieved by doing injustice to no one, equal treatment can only be achieved by not doing anything. With equality we find an idea of justice that immediately brings into focus the idea of freedom. From an etymological point of view 'freedom' is quite different from 'liberty'."

Prof. van Dun further explains the crucial differences between freedom and liberty in a societal context, something many people are perhaps not even aware of -

> "Liberty points to a birth right, an inherent status, or to the status of one who has been adopted as a full member of the family or tribe. As a political term, "liberty" suggests full membership into a political society, and points to notions such as nationality and citizenship."

Freedom on the other hand has entirely different meaning, where stating -

> "The origins of the word 'free' to an old Indian word 'priya' meaning: the self, or one's own, and by extension, what is part of, or related to, or like oneself or what on loves, or holds dear."

While further giving the Latin translation and meaning to be -

"Privatus': one's own, personal, not belonging to the ruler of the state, private."

Given the popular knowledge of how the roots of democracy came from Ancient Greece, van Dun makes mention of how that society attempted to bring freedom under liberty through proponents such as Aristotle in the form of a political society with a unified constitution where van Dun offer the logical retort of the fundamental difference and incompatibility that exists between such legal and lawful standing -

"A constitution (of moral convention) and not by the ties of kinship that define the family and tribal village- may have forged a link between freedom and liberty, but this should not obscure the fundamental distinction. Logically speaking, freedom may well be a ground for claiming liberty to a free person, it does not thereby automatically deprive him of his freedom."

Saying further of constitution -

"Constitution convention grants liberty to a person, it does not automatically make him more free than he was before. The granting of him liberty gives him full membership and status in the constituted political organization, and nothing more - Freedom belongs to the natural being, liberty to a role player, a functionary in an organization. In modern terms, we might say, that liberty belongs to the "public sphere" (i.e. to one's involvement with the business of the state), while freedom belongs to the "private sphere" where people meet one another as free natural persons with full responsibility for their own actions, and not as legal or fictional persons ("citizens") who are likely to explain and justify their actions in terms of legally or constitutionally conferred powers and privileges."

It cannot be stressed how important this information is, and for those who haven't yet comprehended to please read it again, and as many times necessary for this is evidence of the fact that there exists a legal reality in which we are classified as citizens "born into bondage" having a mainstream academic expert in law acknowledge it so, and as further case studies to be examined will plausibly argue, that through the means of the Birth Certificate and further on through having a Social Security number, tax file number and registering to vote are proof of the fact that when we are born into the jurisdiction of a particular constitution thus we become subject to its rules of which we have very little say and further evidence of the reasons why natural law has deliberately been forgotten and Common law become more and more systematized and commercialized.

Such revelations certainly place a different spin on the popular understandings of what being a citizen really means, as well as what a constitution truly stands for, contrary to that propagated in popular history and education, granted both have their uses and benefits, essentially witholding certain true and natural freedoms in place of controlled benefits.

MILITARISTIC GOVERNMENT AND COMMERCE

The language of law and place of origin prove hugely helpful in regards to understanding the legal reality. Remembering of the fact that Civil law having origins in the Roman Empire was in part an aggressive geopolitical outlook, of which the previous quote from 'Historical Jurisprudence' by Guy Carlton Lee plausibly postulates their legal and political language to be also only later to permeate the Common law system of England along with the Babylonian equity and debt practices detailed in the Norman Invasion, later spreading throughout the Commonwealth Empire in the centuries to follow and finally to the modern age to the U.S. Of this postulation, van Dun offers insight in regards to related key words-

> 'Organic freedom is indeed the substance of (subjective) right. Here we should note only that the word 'right' is nowadays understood mainly as referring to elements in a real or ideal legal system. Not surprisingly, it has acquired excessively normative overtones: a right is what the law says, or ought to say, it has lost all descriptive content. The word 'right' when shorn of the current overgrowth of legal and normative meanings, evokes the drama of the struggle against a hostile environment; it conjures up an image of force, manipulating things and subjugating people. Might gives right."

Whereas the more natural context and application as would be found in a Natural/Common law based society they explain to be -

> "We may well ask how this extremely physical concept of right-as-might can be connected to justice. As we use the words 'right', 'recht', 'droit', 'diritto' now, the original meaning has almost completely vanished. The focus has shifted to the latin 'ius', i.e. a moral or social bond, committing oneself and waiting for him to commit himself, one treats him as one's like being mutually independent."

Such fundamental differences as van Dun further demonstrate carry through into the conducting of actions and affairs-

"Even if we disregard the aspects of physical force and violence in the practice of ruling (regnum), we should not overlook the difference between speech by which ones obligates oneself (swearing, promising) and speech by which one obligates others (commanding)."

Being that the Roman Empire ruled aggressively by standing armies (as well as bread and circuses) and through dictatorial Emperors who's word was law reflects in their Civil (legal) language and having carried through into the modern legal lexicon as used by dominant western powers of the modern age, proving to be just as militaristic in nature and structure with such titles and positions as Officer and General and a self-evident history of aggressive domestic and foreign policies of often constant war mongering over diplomacy as well the commercial connection and behavior of corporations being equally aggressive in their conduct through such descriptions as hostile take over's, beating the competition and corporate espionage etc.

Prof. van Dun provides a justifiable summation of which -

"Perhaps the positivistic current in thinking about law harks back to the original idea of right-is-might, and to its application in the form of ' leges' to human material. This would explain its fascination with the phenomena of power and its almost total neglect of questions of 'ius'."

Another reoccurring pattern again comes into view, having studied the Vatican and the history of the Roman Catholic Church having felt justified in its actions by some seemingly higher law and purpose spurred by infallible and Divine right, and so it is here in the modern legal reality we see the powers that be behave likewise from 'their' divine right, coveted and practiced with equally unquestioned and unshakable faith of origin, and apparent right of place.

COMMERCIAL CODES FOR A COMMERCIAL WORLD

The 1930s saw an unprecedented change in government, finance and thus the global socioeconomic system as we know it, where credit and securities became the new means under which all further banking and commerce would take place.

Before the 1930s as is popularly known, governments and banks operated on a gold backed standard up until that time. The banking powers being dissatisfied with the level of profit making from their practices through negotiable instruments and bills of exchange wanted to expand their breath of influence and create more wealth through diversified financial instruments. Industrialists and entrepreneurs likewise sought to create new global scale markets and trade.

With the bank of International settlements (BIS) set in place in 1930 to become the 'central banks of central banks' by promoting the cooperation of central banks and provide additional facilities for international financial operations during WW2, and perhaps a little known fact that it was used by all countries in the war for their financial transactions during the conflict and later used as a key brain trust to coordinate the creation of the global fiat money system of today and enjoys unique and similar status of diplomatic immunity only had by heads of the U.N and IMF. The great depression was orchestrated as the event to flip the switch and reset the system to credit and securities. After 'the roaring twenties' all corporations and governments would operate under this system across the globe.

In 1933 the Securities Act was passed in the U.S. followed by the establishing of the Federal Securities and Exchange Commission and the passing of the Securities Exchange Act both in 1934 as measures to regulate the stock market and prevent further crashes, yet to this day hardly seems effective[25] as well as its attempts to prevent the bribing of foreign officials by

---

[25] Is the SEC Covering Up Wall Street Crimes? www.rollingstone.com /politics/news/is-the-sec-covering-up-wall-street-crimes-20110817

U.S. Corporations abroad in obtaining contracts and money laundering since the 1970s through the Foreign Corrupt Practices Act (FCPA). [26]

If recent demonstrations are anything to go by the events surrounding the withdrawal of gold from circulation in the U.S. from the 'Roosevelt Gold Program' and the Emergency Banking Act in 1933 had global ramifications with loans being called in and trade disrupted in parts of Europe, South American countries, as well as Commonwealth countries such as Australia and New Zealand as a result. All suffered badly between 1931-35 through both trade and unemployment while the system transitioned with Holland being among the last to drop the gold standard. Following World War Two the Bretton Woods conference would take place to establish the U.S. Dollar as the trading currency of the world as well as the birth of the IMF and World Bank, everything was set into place for a future of global socioeconomic control with the U.S. (Federal Reserve) Dollar finally taken off of the gold standard in 1971 while being used as the dominant trading currency of the world since and more importantly that of oil with Saudi Arabia, earning it the well- known nickname of the 'Petro-Dollar'.

Drastic changes had taken place likewise in the legal realm of the 1930s. It was the decade in which the legal system of the U.S. responded to these socioeconomic conditions to the detriment of its people and the western world thereafter. A perfect example to illustrate this change comes from the 1938 court case of Erie Railroad v. Tompkins where a man had sued the Erie Railroad company for damages when struck by a board sticking out of a boxcar while walking alongside the track. The district court ruled that because the man was not under contract with the company he had no standing to sue them. This case was used by a Mr. Howard Freeman in a lecture they gave called *The UCC Connection: Free Yourself from Legal Tyranny* in 1991[27] where they explain the reason why they came across the

---

[26] www.sec.gov /spotlight/fcpa/fcpa-cases.shtml

27 https://ia802707.us.archive.org/35/items/pdfyn30dayZwc0wakHT

case and its significance. After being asked to testify in a tax case for the defendant the judge told the jury they could only decide an outcome on certain facts but none of the ones Freeman had given? He later approached the Judge and asked why they did this. The judge hesitantly explained that the reason being all the facts Freeman had presented where based on cases pre-1938 which up until that time the Supreme court operated under Public (Common) law after which it changed to Public (Commercial law) Policy, the Judge wouldn't say anymore.

The tax case defendant was therefore tried under Public Policy statute not Public law, it was then Freeman began to investigate this change and discovered the Erie Railroad v. Tompkins case and how it was in that year the Federal legal system changed from operating under Common law to Statutory law. Freeman then tells of how they later became friends with the Judge and again asked them of the case, saying they were still confused as to why the Federal system operated under Public Policy and not Public Law. The Judge would reveal, according the Freeman, that in 1938 all the higher Judges along with the top attorneys and U.S. Attorneys were called to a secret meeting to be told America was officially a bankrupt nation owned completely by creditors who in turn owned the Congress, Executive, Judiciary and all state governments.

The aftermath of the Great Depression set in motion three things:

1) The creation of a global fiat currency system by way of credit and implementation of securities to be at the heart of all commerce between and within corporations and countries.

2) The withdrawal of the gold standard leading to the bankruptcy of whole countries across the western world and the U.S. Federal Reserve Dollar emerging as the world's foremost trading currency.

9/Limited%20Liability%20fiat%20paper%20howard%20freeman%20The%20UCC%20Connect
ion%203.30.12%20Coram%20Nobis.pdf

3) Under this new credit and securities system, with the global web of both commercial and central banks set in place under the umbrella of the Bank of International Settlements along with the Securities and Exchange Commission in Washington D.C made western governments register in order to participate in this new global commerce turning them into de facto incorporated entities. Beforehand governments were truly constitutional de jure governments, as well as the case throughout the U.K Commonwealth and countries such as Holland and Spain being Constitutional Monarchs. Other countries as well as these throughout the western sphere would be ruled under Common or Civil law with government being elected to serve as part of a Public Trust with Politicians and government arms such as the Police being public servants to the people. This new socioeconomic system essentially usurped this Trust turning all of it into what has essentially become a commercial operation. The banking powers were now fully in control.

LOST AT SEA

Returning to the relevance of the court case of 1938 in light of the previous chapter can the Judge's decision and his revelations made to Mr. Freeman now be fully comprehended, the world was going commercial and that included the relationship between the public and commerce.

If we recall how the judge in Mr. Freeman's story said the court to be operating under statutory law, be it more specifically what is called Admiralty jurisdiction. Admiralty law also known as Maritime law which generally follows Civil law principles began and still operates as a codified system of private law for maritime activities of transporting goods and passengers by sea, this was later used to cover land-based commercial activities as well in certain aspects of international law between nations as part of numerous multilateral treaties.

The Admiralty/Maritime system works by Admiralty court assuming jurisdiction by virtue of the presence of the 'vessel' in its territorial jurisdiction irrespective of whether the vessel is national or not and whether registered or not, and wherever the residence or domicile or their owners may be, while a vessel is also usually arrested by the court to retain jurisdiction. State-owned vessels are immune from arrest and there exists no grand jury.

Bearing this in mind and given the circumstance of the 1938 court case, the following information will further clarify just why the Judge did not want to initially confess this to Mr. Freeman. In Admiralty law, without a valid international contract dispute there is no jurisdiction established, and therefore if the claim is being made that such a contract exists one can demand it be brought forth and placed into evidence. In the court case the man suing the company didn't have any such grounds there being no contract in place and therefore lost the case.

The aftermath of the Great Depression of the global Credit and Securities system set in motion alterations of western government from de jure to de facto entities and in light of this made operations of court of law commercial instead of natural justice, giving plausible and evidential postulation of the change in nature of relationship having deliberately been made between the people and government ever since, who are to be likewise treated as commercial entities.

Given the evidence of just how severely regulated, taxed and monitored life in the western world has increasingly become is clear that government and the courts operate from Admiralty jurisdiction by enforcing acts and statutes that compel performance with risk of criminal penalties if not followed to the letter. This adoption of Admiralty law is nothing secret yet public ignorance plays to the favour of the establishment of not knowing nor understanding the extent to which it has been used to affect everyday life being blanketed as Statutory law. Everything from parking and speeding fines to paying taxes are acts and statutes that compel performance or risk being penalized such as a hefty fine or going to jail, it has become all about commerce and the generating of revenue. The element of contract is also key to this situation, being a crucial part of the argument presented by movements of those across the west most notably the U.S, Canada, the U.K. and Ireland seeking Natural and Common law solutions and remedies to such enforcement.

Let us now take a further look at the Commercial system of codes that serve as part of the machinery for this global commercial and legal reality and the case study of those having attempted to find remedy within it.

THE UCC AND INTERNATIONAL EQUIVALENTS

With the credit and securities system in place and the implementation of Admiralty jurisdiction a wholly commercial world was in operation by the mid twentieth century. The Government and banking powers now needed a cohesive and codified system of rules to operate it which by no surprise originated in the U.S. known as the UCC (Uniform Commercial Code) as the prime registry of all commercial activity on the planet being that every interconnected nation its government and thus citizens[28] as well as all other legal corporations are registered as commercial 'vessels' essentially to be then bought and sold as assets and interests.

Since its creation in the 1950s to harmonize commercial transactions across the U.S. the UCC has evolved into a vast network of International, national and state portals as well as branches and franchises which are then funneled and consolidated into the major portal of Washington D.C and registered with the Federal SEC (Securities and Exchange Commission) to be further listed on the International Stock Markets and other major business listing companies such as Dunn & Bradstreet in the U.K. A complex and encrypted system of number coding is then used by stock brokerages and traders to identify whatever type of commercial instrument 'vessels' may be such as Mortgages and other types of Trusts and Securities to be bought and sold. We will explore more on this process a bit later.

The international equivalents to the UCC have been in development through trade treaties over the course of the twentieth century such as through NAFTA with Canada being among the first to adopt the system in 1967 later to be called the PPSA (Personal Property Securities Act) and Quebec also having its own equivalent though being under French Civil law. In Common law jurisdictions of the U.K. and its Commonwealth territories of Hong Kong and Singapore as well as Ireland operate through a Charges register, a

---

[28] Controversial yet strongly plausible through means of the Birth Certificate registration process and other means of becoming warded to the state such as social security and registering to vote, all of which will be examined in the final section of this work.

charge being the name of security given as a loan by companies and registered at a Company house or Lender agent. All share the similarity of being conducted through a Companies Act. This system also ties into land registry throughout these territories. New Zealand adopted the Canadian PPSA in the Nineties with Australia adopting it as recent as 2012.

Civil law jurisdictions are quite different and a bit more complex in the case of filing securities and liens, the key difference being a filing is made against the actual asset and not the title to the asset as with Common law countries. Things such as land, patents and trademarks being among those having specific registers. Throughout this system however are complications such as location of an asset, location of the title, asset holder as well as type of jurisdiction requiring case-by-case analysis due to the complicated variety of transactions that arise and the uses of filing procedure known as the law of perfection.

Both the UN and EU have found inspiration from the UCC by adopting similar rules to their own mandates with the United Nations Legislative guide on Secured Transactions, the European Draft Common Frame of Reference (DCFR) and the European Bank of Reconstruction and Development's model law on secured transactions.

DO YOU SPEAK COMMERCIAL CODE?

The Banking Industry with the Securitization process has its own language. Some of the specific language associated with the Banks and the Securitization process includes the following terms:

- Offering
- Circular
- RMBS's
- CBS's
- ROAP's
- Conduits
- Payflo
- Tender
- Code
- Master
- Trust
- Custodian
- Servicing

- BOSS
- FASIT
- FICO
- TCODE
- TALF
- TILA
- Tranche
- CUSIP
- Clearstream
- Note Prospectus
- Rider
- Amortisation
- General Ledger .

These are good search terms for further investigative learning. Let us now take a look at one example of the CUSIP system[29] (Committee on Uniform Security Identification Procedures) and the primary unique identifier used for US bonds started in 1964. The system is owned by the American Bankers Association, and administered by Standard and Poor's. There are CUSIP numbers for most US traded securities while also being used in the bond market to process and settle trades. The CUSIP identifier consists of nine characters: a base number of six characters known as the issuer identifier, the 4th, 5th and/or 6th position of which may be alpha or numeric and a two-character suffix. The number is generated by what is known as the 'Modulus 10 Double Add Double' technique to assign each CUSIP a security identifier.

---

29 https://www.cusip.com/pdf/CUSIP_Intro_03.14.11.pdf

Issuer Identifier 837649

8	3	7	6	4	9
X1	X2	X2	X2	X1	X2
8	6	12	12	4	18

Issuer Identifier 12

1	2
X1	X2
1	4

Thus 8+6+7+1+2+4+1+8+1+4=42

The CUSIP identifier with optional check digit would then be 837649 12 8

Another widely used identification coding system is the International Securities Identification Number (ISIS) being adopted by the G30 in 1989. The ISIN code is a 12-character alphanumerical code. It does not contain information that characterizes financial instruments but is used for uniform identification of a security through normalization of the assigned National Number for trading and settlement. Securities that use the ISIS include debt securities, shares, options, derivatives and futures.

Just as an example of how deep the profit motive goes and the competitive greed which permeates this commercial framework, in 2009 the firm Standard & Poor's were charged by the European Commission (EC) for abusing its position as the sole provider of international securities identification codes for United States of America securities by requiring European financial firms and data vendors to pay licensing fees for their use, obviously not happy enough with making millions per annum in commission already.

MUNICIPAL BONDS-STREETS PAVED WITH GOLD?

As another interesting aside, if even further proof were needed to confirm the fully commercialized nature of government, though again no secret is the activity of Municipal Bond trading in the U.S. [30] otherwise known as local authority bond trading elsewhere with the U.K, Sweden, Finland and New Zealand. It actually has roots as early as the European Renaissance and first began in the U.S. in the 1800s. It is primarily a means for both National and local government as well as other agencies to finance public projects such as roads, schools, airports and seaports, and other infrastructure related projects and repairs while easing the need to raise taxes.

Interestingly some economists praise the idea[31] as a solution to government deficit while dealing with the issue of low corporate tax rates on multinationals as a way to retain their business and not fleeing to other, typically developing, countries by offering them municipal shares instead of charging higher taxes. This could also be part of the solution to tax havens.

---

[30] https://www.wellscap.com/pdf/expert_commentary/non_us_investors_muni_bonds.pdf

[31] http://www.independent.ie/opinion/columnists/david-mcwilliams/david-mcwilliams-eu-is-a-thing-of-the-past-our-future-is-with-an-atlantic-ireland-35009330.html

THE COMMERCIAL CITY STATE CONNECTION

While researching the UCC system it was discovered that it has a procedure called 'Cross-border financing' for debtors overseas if an asset were located in the U.S. which allows the filing location to be wherever the debtor is of which the District of Colombia is classified to be outside of the U.S.

For those unaware the District of Colombia like the Vatican state and City of London is an independent city-state. Is it any coincidence that each are significant and respective consolidations of religious, political and financial power while being independent to the laws of the territories they dwell within? Yet ultimately affect the socioeconomic health of those territories while remaining above and outside of their laws. Is it any wonder then why Admiralty jurisdiction is so favoured by the political and financial powers located therein, as it operates regardless of location, of the number of parties involved or assets in question thus making it the perfect form of international commercial Law.

We can see clearly now why international trade treaties are continuously being refined and expanded so as to streamline this process into more and more territories making for the perfect mechanism of global commercial control, effectively becoming a one world government, all the while being under the umbrella of the global banking system spearheaded by the Bank of International Settlements (BIC) also an entity with its own powers of impunity located in Switzerland.

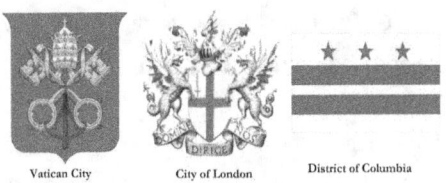

| Vatican City | City of London | District of Columbia |

The City States and their insignia

THE CASE OF THE OPPT

On December the 25th of 2012 a small group of people formed what was called the OPPT (One People's Public Trust) consisting of Caleb Skinner, Hollis Randall Hillner and Heather Ann Tucci-Jaraf announcing to the world the legal foreclosure of all Corporations, Banks and Governments through a series of UCC filings. This they claimed forced the global corporate system into foreclosure and by their failure to rebut this claim now stands as law, stating further that through international law the OPPT exercised the right to claim remedy on behalf of 'the One People' which included reclaiming all assets and infrastructures as well as all gold and silver held by all commercial and central banks. As a former lawyer who dealt in UCC Heather Ann Tucci-Jaraf spearheaded the initiative, even going so far as to use the foreclosure of their home as a test case challenging it through UCC processes, but found the court system to act in conflict of interest by ruling in favour of the banks despite being in the right, proving the system was inherently biased and corrupt.

All three members claimed themselves to be Trustees of this trust bonding every individual on the planet to the trust as beneficiaries in equity in their UCC filings demonstrated in the following pages hence calling it "The One People, created by the Creator" stating they were effectively resuming the trust framed in the original U.S. Constitution of 1776 abandoned by the Federal government after becoming corporatized in 1933. By building upon the Constitution with these new terms of the trust that encompassed all of humanity under God/a Creator, they state, then made it lawfully superior to an Act, Statute or de facto corporate government entity.

They set about lodging their filings between 2011 and 2012 with the documents available for reading on their website[32] although caution is advised as it makes for heavy legal and technical reading to a nonprofessional. They explain the process in summary to be, that they filed

---

32 http://i-uv.com

an "Order of Finding and Action" against "the debtor" being a legal entity created using the UCC process to be all corporate entities with the claim that the debtor –

> "Knowingly, willingly and intentionally committed treason by owning, operating, aiding and abetting private money systems as well as "Operating slavery systems used against citizens without their willing and intentional consent."

Given that the UCC process is fully public as part of its operations requiring transparency with communication between parties, the entities (debtors) had full knowledge and notification of OPPT's claims while having the right of rebuttal and if not received within a certain timeframe a default action follows along with the termination of that entity. This they state gives conclusive proof that the filing worked as they have yet to be rebutted, therefore the follow through being the case, that all debt be erased and all wealth of the planet returned to "the One People". They then stated it now stands as international law with the public record to prove it.

Shortly after in 2013 OPPT for obvious reasons received a frenzy of mixed enthusiasm and skepticism among the online alternative media community with radio shows and websites featuring a barrage of interviews, opinions and reviews. A list of frequently asked questions was released soon after to explain the process and demystify any confusion. Among the questions being, that how can individuals be bonded to the OPPT without their express consent, what of the rumors on the internet that the OPPT wasn't lawful and what will become of society now that all government and corporations had been shut down.

The OPPT again explained that once the UCC filing was unable to be rebutted, thus remaining as law and being it is a Trust did not require expressed consent, only rebuttal to invalidate it and furthermore being the free and unimpeded will of every being is protected by the terms of the OPPT, which leads to another area of interest, some of which will be examined a little later but for the moment to say involves the case of personal responsibility and dealing with other parties, being that OPPT having foreclosed all government, banking and commercial entities means that there is no longer the legal mechanism or corporate protocols in place for other parties to hide behind making everyone free and willing to be self-accountable, not unlike a fundamental principle of Natural law. As for the rumours that OPPT isn't lawful they explain how those of the OPPT specifically Heather Tucci-Jarraf being a lawyer both familiar and practiced in UCC can verify this not to be true having the knowledge and experience to 'frame' the UCC filings so as to know how to use the system against the Powers that be, and therefore having had the documents successfully filed and accepted and so standing as international law, the manner of which they explain being the equivalent of a criminal indictment against the system.

What will become of society next is perhaps the most open ended question and one that could be answered in two parts, the first being the case of self- accountability and secondly accountability for the planet, and where the opportunity and means to do so, as what solutions such as what the OPPT has provided. For the present time responders to the actions taken by OPPT since 2012 have further asked if this has taken place why then are we not seeing any obvious proof both locally and internationally?

Again a two-part answer is required, the first being to consider that obviously the powers that be aren't going to just stop and admit what is happening, that business as usual will continue so no sudden outward events are going to occur overnight the powers that be will continue to try and ignore this, should we be surprised how much arrogance and ego play into all this. Secondly, having set all this in motion the OPPT guys look now to have played their part having given the means for the rest of us to take initiative and self-accountability by how we go about bringing change. One of the main mean this can be done is through the process of a Courtesy Notice. The following comes from the OPPT archive website *i-uv.com* regarding the process in relation to OPPT and the UCC outcomes and good background on CNs for those who don't know what it is –

> "A Courtesy Notice (CN) is an offer to contract, sent by you to an individual in a bank, corporation or government. It is sent in response to a letter of demand, a threat of action, a summons, or other unlawful demand, detention or arrest – some tangible thing that is causing you harm.

Firstly, the Courtesy Notice alerts that person to the foreclosure of their bank, company or government, resulting from filings by the OPPT. Secondly it informs that individual that henceforth they now act in full personal liability and can no longer 'hide' behind the former entity.

Thirdly, the CN offers that individual a choice; to do nothing, or to continue the action as though nothing had changed. Please understand that this choice is not offered to the foreclosed entity, but solely to the individual who still believes that the entity (his/her employer) has the authority to continue the harmful action against you.

That individual is named as "the Respondent" on the CN, which is addressed with that individual's name c/- of the [alleged Corporate Name, alleged Bank or alleged Company] You are identified as the "Proponent".

The Courtesy Notice IS NOT A NOTICE OF DEMAND. To do so would be the equivalent of YOU operating a "slavery System" – which is exactly what the courtesy notice exposes as "foreclosed".

The Courtesy Notice does "order" that the action against you (by the entity) be CEASED AND DESISTED, but also offers terms and conditions that will apply if the action is continued by the Respondent (individual).

Accordingly, the CN is an offer of contract – based on your terms and conditions. The respondent has a choice. Please make sure you have a copy of the Courtesy Notice Guidelines with you, as you are customizing your CN's, to follow along as a checklist. Choose from the following CN templates, depending on the action being taken against you or/and any action you wish to further prevent."

The i-uv.com website also has a section for success stories but upon visiting and perusing them could not see any conclusive or successful stories of ceasing to pay a mortgage or continue to receive utilities such as water and electricity without having to pay for them, although some success stories mentioned getting rid of debt collectors for loans and credit cards but solutions already exist for these things outside of OPPT's framework.

84

Despite the level of alternative media attention, they received until what looks to be up until 2014 from the list of radio podcasts on the i-uv.com website. At the time of writing I only had time to listen to a number which consisted of members only continuing to discuss the more metaphysical and quasi-spiritual aspects of the philosophy behind the OPPT and less about technical legal aspects or events, though one quote found in this regard they state if challenged of the validity of the UCC filings to respond –

"...a duly verified rebuttal of the DECLARATION OF FACTS UCC#2012127914, point by point, with specificity and particularity by duly sworn declaration, with their full responsibility and liability, under penalty of perjury governing law, or any law so long as it is identified, and signed by their wet ink signature."

QUESTIONING THE OPPT

In light of this however the author found a number of questions relative to such practical and everyday situations those behind OPPT have yet been able to answer in the comments section of one of the major alternative media websites 'wakeup-world.com' which featured an article on the OPPT and Frequently asked Questions. The questions raised such concerns as there being no further feedback from those behind OPPT of any mechanisms to enforce the paradigm shift it purports, that despite the filing documents being available for viewing[33] some remain sceptic as well as no mechanism of authority to stop government and corporate powers from continuing on business as usual.

Others doubt the Courtesy Notice method, but seeing that proof is a case-by-case basis issue, leaves room for confirmation and being a real and tangible experience to those who undertake it and is an on-going thing with Facebook OPPT online communities.[34] As well as of course the big questions of what happens if one were to just stop paying rent or a mortgage and the sheriff or bailiff show up with a bank rep to evict, handing them a courtesy notice may still land you in jail, what if no one went to work with no guarantee to receive any remuneration to live, a courtesy notice won't help there either. What will happen to those who depend on Social Welfare or Disability benefits, as well as proof of any success by the OPPT initiators themselves.

Apart from the explanation given of the filing process and evidence of said documents others remained unconvinced and wished to see proof of being officially accepted by a legal or contesting body as well as proof of document rulings made by a court or governing body. Also proof of official legal documents that record that the contested parties are no longer legally in effect, with evidence of procedures undertaken by OPPT under UCC law

---

33 http://i-uv.com/oppt-absolute/original-oppt-ucc-filings/

34 https://www.facebook.com/groups/177354775749326/

that have made their legal actions effective and complete documentation of their efforts.

Other worthwhile questions for reasonable doubt ask why are the OPPT's documents filed with New Age jargon? Despite having to be legally accepted arguably weaken the credibility and integrity of the whole initiative. Also the apparent paradox that if their filings have foreclosed all government and therefore all legal framework, and since UCC operates in said framework doesn't that then nullify the filing? Others also took issue with having no input in the process or how it was worded.

In the case of Compensation for no longer having a means of income as complained about by some. The OPPT proposed the development what they describe as a replacement system of governance called 'Creators Value Asset Centres or CVACs. Of which they claimed. An explanation described as follows –

> "The CVAC system is the antithesis of the corrupt, externally controlled looting devices that were termed Governments. They are in fact, in commerce, in law, preserved by public policy, REGISTERED as wholly owned, with full title, value and rights, co-jointly and equally by each of the one people on this planet, expressly warranted to be entirely transparent entities that exist only to serve the people of this planet by providing any systems of assistance the people of this planet deem necessary or desired, and these systems are prevented from impinging on any aspect of the free will of any human."

Further information was sought from available web addresses at the time of writing in 2016 only to find the domains up for sale. The following statement was later found made by the trio from sometime in 2013 featured on another website in the course of research as the original link was no longer working, thankfully a member of this other website posted what gives a fitting summation to this whole event, in their own words –

> "OPPT Dissolved March 18! Thank You for your Service. The OPPT held space for the One People for a period of 90 days. The OPPT gracefully served its purpose. It awoke, empowered, and activated the people. Its job has been fulfilled. It is NOW up to the People, as I, Universal Value embodied absent all limits,

themselves.- Over the period of three years, OPPT Trustees Heather Ann Tucci-Jarraf, Caleb Skinner and Hollis Randall Hillner diligently researched, investigated and created the OPPT by learning through personal experience that the root of the corrupt system had its origins within with the Uniform Commercial Code (UCC). They came to know that the system had been crafted by a few powerful individuals to intentionally, perpetually, financially enslave humankind. The UCC filings made by the trustees, through the OPPT, dealt the final death blow to these Powers That Were, foreclosing upon all corporations, including corporations masquerading as "governments". This vital and essential act helped to awaken the populace to the fact that their world reality was quite different than what they had been lead to believe."

Since the initial excitement surrounding the launch of OPPT in 2013/14 Alternative media attention seems to have died down as well as any real or consistent coverage or activity from figures within the Alternative community. The original trio of Caleb Skinner, Hollis Randall Hillner and Heather Ann Tucci-Jaraf have since been working on a next stage of the OPPT concept of which the same website source explains –

"The I U/V Exchange (formally known as OPPT) is the NOW-level evolution as the embodiment of true value. OUR true value as the ABSOLUTE embodiment of Eternal Essence, absent all limits, is infinite. Within this New Paradigm, the concept of money and exchange requires a redefinition. As each person's value of their BEing is infinite, money becomes a distraction from their true worth of DOing and BEing. Bob Wright announced on the Gwen Caldwell Morning Brew show on April 17, 2013 that former trustee Caleb Skinner is currently working on the new system, that it is nearly complete. - The April 18, 2013 Morning Brew Show with Brian Kelly and Bob Wright expounds upon the newest evolutions of the system, OPPT being approached by the SWISSINDO group, the United Nations (UN) involvement, Provosts arrests, etc, and up-to-the minute evolutions of the I/UV exchange. It has become glaringly apparent that we need a bridge to bring us to where we are going. We are creating our new paradigm as we progress within each NOW moment."

After researching about this new development[35] at face value appeared to be a mix of metaphysical/ quasi-spiritual and legal aspects in form, which again may not be to everyone's liking never the less still attracts an audience of spectators and volunteers alike seeking freedom from the establishment, the foreseeable future of which could prove interesting and potentially be among solutions of transition to a NLRBE.

---

35 http://i-uv.com/i-uv/i-and-the-uv-exchange/

THE THING ABOUT TRUSTS

The founders of OPPT and now with their latest development of the 'I U/V Exchange' have perhaps done themselves no favours in attaching metaphysical and quasi-spiritual inclinations to its mandate with some people just wanting real and practical solutions and not some belief system that now that we have the means to believe and claim everything will work out in our favour because it is being done so under a benevolent Creator/God.

However, as an aside, keeping things in the lawful realm and remembering that Constitutions are indeed founded under 'God' ideally should work in our favour in getting out from under this tyrannical framework. Lawfully speaking God is logically the highest law, followed by man who then created the legal system so therefore Gods law trumps man made law, so no man should really have the right to oppress another, but of course things have gotten so far away from this fundamental truth as examined in the section on differences between lawfulness and legality, with Government having more and more deliberately become a corporatized entity for oppression of the people through divisive legal frameworks coupled with the debt and credit based commercial system and not what it was intended to be, a servant of the people.

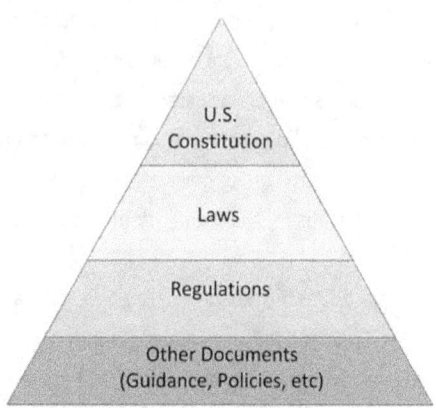

**The legal and lawful hierarchy
Constitutions and Common Laws
though higher in importance have been
Hijacked and suppressed by man made
regulations of Acts, Statutes and Policies
.i.e the Legal Reality**

The work of OPPT also caught the attention and criticism of others regarding Trust law namely a veteran researcher in Trust Law Australian Frank O' Collins who has been studying and lecturing on the Roman Civil and Canon law systems for over twenty years. There criticisms of the OPPT[36] were on the grounds of being unlawful, as despite their being Trustees and Beneficiaries a Trust needs to have a Grantor, this wasn't specified with the OPPT, and is important as the Grantor is also the owner of the property in question.

One other veteran researcher from the U.S. Winston Shrout explained also reasons why the OPPT doesn't work from a legal standpoint either.[37] They clarify how first of all there is a difference between filing and recording within the UCC system and secondly within the U.S. there is a

---

36 https://anticorruptionsociety.com/tag/frank-ocollins/

37 https://anticorruptionsociety.com/2013/02/27/one-peoples-public-trust-buyer-beware/

difference between doing this at a State and National level, saying the mistake the OPPT made was filing a National form and not a State level recording, as filing is only a notice which in legal terms means only taking an interest in the thing your filing in aid of, whereas recording is making an actual lien (financing statement) and expressing a security interest in something. Therefore, filing is not taking control of property.

Shrout also point out the importance of language being fundamental and paramount within the legal system, where the OPPT said they had foreclosed on all governments and corporations Shrout says to be misleading as it has multiple meanings and connections in regards to legal processes. Saying also the conclusions behind the OPPT's actions and reasons as to be incorrect concepts, being that those behind it elected themselves to be Trustees without the express consent of those to be the Beneficiaries, the people. Over all they say it to be too ambitious, misguided and impractical both in scope and scale.

Two questions arise from this: How could there be contradictions in the process of establishing the Trust where Shrout states, they weren't allowed to self- nominate as the Trustees and yet if we recall from the frequently asked questions of people asking this very question, the answer stated they could only if not rebutted?

Secondly, is the broader issue of the recording and filing differences within the UCC system, as well as Shrout's explanation of being done incorrectly, indicating that perhaps to be just a process within the U.S? That despite the understanding from the research made by this author and statements from the OPPT of the UCC operating with and through other international equivalents, and as they stated a lodgment in one portal is as good as a lodgment with any, being after all an international system. The UCC lodging process apparently will only work within the territorial jurisdiction of the U.S.

For the moment these questions and contradictions have reached an impasse. We will leave this topic for now, but further study and questioning are worthwhile to see if this method could one day prove useful and validated among the means to transition to a NLRBE. If anything, even if mistaken the case study of the OPPT has helped open more doors in understanding over all the global legal and commercial framework.

THE SISTERS IN LAW

In its irony to have complete control empires always appear to display a weakness for centralized and singular congregation, and structural administration. In the Introduction by Julian Assange of the book *'The Wikileaks Files'* give the following insightful commentary fitting to this situation–

> "The study of empires has long been the study of their communications. Carved into stone or inked on parchment, empires from Babylon to the Ming Dynasty left records of the organizational centre communicating with its peripheries. However, by the 1950s students of historical empires realized that somehow the communications medium was the empire. Its methods for organizing the inscriptions, transportation, indexing and storage of its communications, and for designating who was authorized to read and write them, in a real sense constituted the empire."

A further study of the global legal/commercial system of the UCC and its equivalents would indeed be very useful but for the moment is beyond the scope of this work. From the strong evidence having been gleaned.

The system works essentially by de facto (corporate) governments, major banking trusts, holding companies and other subsidiaries registering in Washington D.C through the Federal SEC system to be then traded on the global stock exchange through various securities, but who authorizes and administers the legal framework to make this work between territories.

Yet who are the legal experts and facilitators? The following examples were found to be a good starting point in understanding.

The modern legal reality is evidently a modern empire and international trade/commercial law being among the means to which it exists and perpetuate. Those who create and administer it may have changed hands many times having grown that much larger and more diversified over time but the system remains; the idea is essentially the same, a system of control, on top of which is cascading in nature and pyramidal in nature consisting of hierarchical sub systems within parent systems.

The following are three of the most prominent bodies having been established to monitor and administer this global empire, being **UNCITRAL, UNIDROIT** and **The Hague Conference on Private International Law**, known in circles as 'the Three Sisters'. The first of which is the core legal body of the United Nations established over 40 years with an international membership and offices in the UN HQ of New York and the International Centre in Vienna. Its main function is to oversee and resolve any disputes between members in the continued modernization and harmonization of the rules of international business. It does so through the use of conventions, model laws and rules accepted worldwide as well as legal and legislative guides and other recommendations of valued practice, to provide technical and professional assistance in law reform projects around the world, and last but not least to maintain updated information on case law and enactments of UCC (Uniform Commercial Code) Law. Such areas covered under these headings include International Commercial Arbitration and Conciliation, procurement and infrastructural development, international sales of goods and transportation and other related transactions, Security Interests, Insolvency, payments, E-Commerce and other online dispute resolutions.

The International Institute of the Unification of private Law (UNIDROIT) is an intergovernmental organization established in Rome in 1926 describing itself at the time to be 'an auxiliary organ of the League of Nations' and re-established in 1940 after the league collapse operating through multilateral agreement with client States. It remains as a private and independent entity for the purpose of being able to adopt working methods they describe to be 'less political and more technical' in nature for various issues. Among its services it provides the formulating of uniform law instruments that are adopted under the auspices of other international organizations including the preparation of comparative law studies as well as to draft Conventions designed to accompany these under the headings of principles and rules for the modernizing, harmonizing and coordination of private and commercial law between States and groups of States. At present it has a count of 63 member states that also provide operating funds along with an annual contribution from the Italian government.

The Hague Conference on Private International Law describes itself to be not just a facilitator of relationships between States but rather the lives of their citizens, private and commercial, in cross-border relationships and transactions and by which its task and purpose being to develop and service frameworks of multilateral legal instruments which, despite the differences between legal systems will allow individuals as well as companies to enjoy a high degree of legal security. The Hague Conference being the oldest of these bodies established in 1893 as a center resolution for numerous and historical resolution disputes has served as the deciding ground in the recognition and adoption of the world's two most prominent systems of law in Common and Civil law, in terms of which law to apply and in which jurisdiction, resolutely devising a system to accommodate both as they describe[38] -

> "For the service of process abroad and for the taking of evidence abroad; to reconcile different conceptions of the succession of estates of deceased persons and the administration of such estates; and to recognise the institution of the trust, widely used in the common law world but practically unknown in civil law systems."

With the continuing growth of signatures, ratifications and accessions to The Hague Conventions, 129 States in all parts of the world are now connected to The Hague Conference, either as Member States or as Parties to one or more of the Hague Conventions which are also open to non-Member States of the Organisation.

Headings under which conventions have been drawn up in its history do include matters of International legal co-operation and litigation as well as judicial and administrative co-operation and enforcement of

---

[38] HAGUE JUSTICE JOURNAL I JOURNAL JUDICIAIRE DE LA HAYE VOLUME/VOLUME 2 I NUMBER/ NUMÉRO 2 I 2007

judgments. International Commercial and Finance law for Contracts, Torts, Securities and Trusts, and quite significantly 'Recognition of Companies' passed in June of 1956 on the Recognition of the Legal Personality of Foreign Companies, Associations and Foundations, as well as the issue of International family and property relations covering International protection of Children, of Adults, of relations between (former) spouses and finally Wills, Estates and Trusts. The current status of signatures, ratifications and accessions can be seen here.[39] Although a venue of facilitation The Hague does not have the authority to enforce conventions nor promulgate regulations or directives, member states remain free and independent to recognize or ignore them and are further only recognized through constitutional procedure. Often is the case that members don't fully adopt conventions but take into practice only certain or some of its rules, using The Hague Convention as a model for their own such as with the EU. It could say to have far more serious recognition among authorities and courts throughout the world than political governments to create and facilitate cross-border and cross-party communication and cooperation among courts in the different member states.[40]

As before mentioned with the world having become more and more complex so too has the legal reality. Institutions such as the three sisters are proof of which and crucial in handling the workload. The Hague Conference describes itself to be in increasingly higher demand with the exponential growth in the field of regional and globalized international trade law to facilitate globalization, a history of which shows to be anything but perfect in regards to international environmental and human rights violations abound.

---

[39] http://www.hcch.net/upload/statmtrx_e.pdf

[40] www.incadat.com

ARBITRATING THE SYSTEM

The primary purpose of these three facilitators is to maintain modernization and harmonization between parties. While much pomp and ceremony has been given to harmonization between peoples of the world through proclamations, declarations, and charters on human rights and other such issues the commercial realm is where the real resolving of conflict has always mattered most.[41] Trade indeed dictates everything material in this world it seems; from the if and when of war[42] or the strength and effectiveness of diplomacy among countries to the everyday quality of life for millions within those countries while underlined by the health, wealth and management of global environments.

If we recall, the mention and brief examination of how the global legal and commercial framework came about after the events of the 1930s there has followed a consistent history of trade and diplomacy conventions and treaties to harmonize trade between territories and although, as we now know of, the UCC and its global equivalents being set in place to facilitate such things, are far from perfect or harmonious. Those in power in all levels of the system throughout all territories who wish to have absolute success in the implentation of this legal and commercial empire are in fact a fractious and self-interested lot, with their own self-serving agendas and ideals of how it should work and run. We can now see why harmonization of legal frameworks, conventions and treaties are ongoing in order to have any form of cooperation and why there are parent and independent facilitating institutions such as the UN and the UNITRAL to maintain consistent order.

A major issue of contention of late is the suing of governments by multinational corporations. This issue has never been so hotly contested nor debated as with the recent spate of trade deals of the TTP, TTIP and TISA. Although as touched upon earlier that governments certainly in the western

---

[41] www.asia-pacificresearch.com /brics-and-the-fiction-of-de-dollarization/5441787

[42] www.asia-pacificresearch.com /beijing-vs-washington-the-battle-for-southeast-asia-free-trade-and-us- economic-hegemony/5505641

hemisphere among others elsewhere have become de facto and thus corporate in nature and play the commercial game as much as any other corporate and commercial entity, still don't wish to be undermined in their prime purpose as the issuer and governor of laws within their own territories. A mounting body of cases demonstrate how governments are being inhibited in their capacity to legislate environmental, labour and health protection standards at risk of being sued by corporations operating within their territory on the grounds of inhibiting profit making operations.

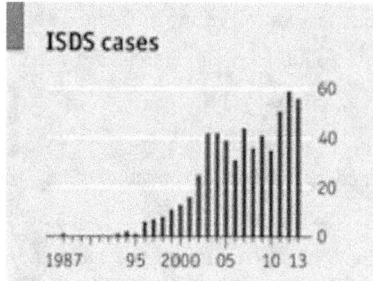

The global exponential rise in ISDS Cases

A key instrument in this is called the Investor-State Dispute Settlement (ISDS) provision. One example of objection to this comes from Australia within the Green party[43] concerning the TTP having obtained the analysis of legal arbitration experts on safeguards for the Australian government and thus the greater welfare of the country to be 'frankly inadequate'. Australian government literature[44] however outlines the ISDS provision of a recent trade deal established with China in 2015 with the China-Australia Free Trade Agreement (ChAFTA) to include safeguards for both parties to include the protection of legitimate government regulation in areas such as public health and the environment to include legitimate public welfare objectives of public health, safety, the environment, public morals or public order as well as to

---

[43] greens.org.au /campaigns/national/stop-tpp

[44] http://dfat.gov.au/trade/topics/pages/isds.aspx

adopt new measures in sensitive areas including with respect to security, human health and creative arts.

The FAQ release from the EU regarding the TTIP[45] attempts to quell public fear and skepticism in regards to corporations being able to sue member governments. Such public backlash is understandable considering the secrecy of the matter even for MEPs (Members of the European Parliament) up until August of 2015 when only certain sections were disclosed for their perusal under supervision, but as of December 2015 [46] have been given full access open for debate. Perhaps the actions of Wikileaks[47] along with internal and external public pressures had forced the hand of its creators to give full disclosure in attempts to demystify the situation, and finally to much public outcry and relief abandonment of the TTIP being announced in 2016. One of the key questions of course being would the ISDS prevent governments from regulating the TTIP in favour of public interests i.e. can they be sued? The answer being no, that the EU had been working with the UN to develop a more transparent system of resolving investor dispute settlements[48] and protections while outlining rights and conduct to both parties with the inclusion of an appeals process.

---

[45] http://ec.europa.eu/trade/policy/in-focus/ttip/about-ttip/questions-and-answers/

[46] http://www.europarl.europa.eu/news/de/news-room/20151202IPR05759/all-meps-to-have-access-to-all-confidential-ttip-documents

[47] https://wikileaks.org/WikiLeaks-goes-after-hyper-secret.html

[48] www.uncitral.org /uncitral/uncitral_texts/arbitration/2014Transparency_FAQ.html

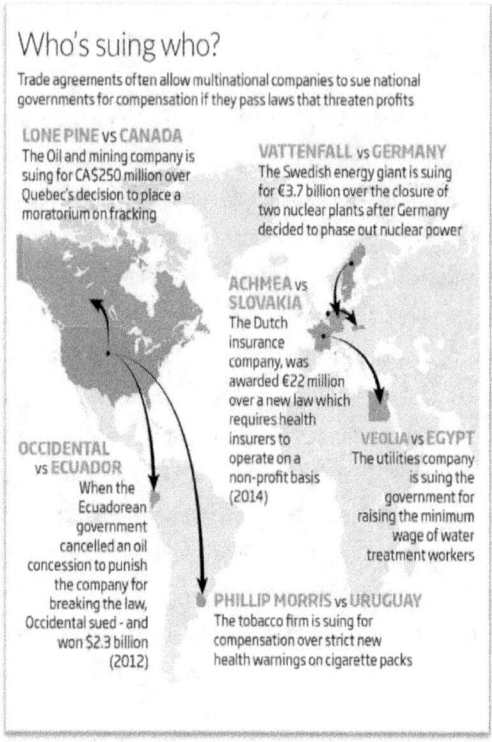

Who's suing who?

Trade agreements often allow multinational companies to sue national governments for compensation if they pass laws that threaten profits

LONE PINE vs CANADA
The Oil and mining company is suing for CA$250 million over Quebec's decision to place a moratorium on fracking

VATTENFALL vs GERMANY
The Swedish energy giant is suing for €3.7 billion over the closure of two nuclear plants after Germany decided to phase out nuclear power

ACHMEA vs SLOVAKIA
The Dutch insurance company, was awarded €22 million over a new law which requires health insurers to operate on a non-profit basis (2014)

OCCIDENTAL vs ECUADOR
When the Ecuadorean government cancelled an oil concession to punish the company for breaking the law, Occidental sued - and won $2.3 billion (2012)

VEOLIA vs EGYPT
The utilities company is suing the government for raising the minimum wage of water treatment workers

PHILLIP MORRIS vs URUGUAY
The tobacco firm is suing for compensation over strict new health warnings on cigarette packs

Governments and Corporations suing one another have become
a present day norm

The vehicle for this reform the EU propose will be called 'The Investment Court System' replacing the existing ISDS mechanism in regard to the TTIP as a result of decisions arrived at from input from the European Parliament, Member States, National Parliaments among members and other stakeholders and will include many of the elements of law of domestic and international courts, as described to then 'enshrine government right to regulate and ensure transparency and accountability.' The new court will have what is described as a 'first instance Tribunal and Appeal Tribunal' set up with the establishment of publicly appointed judges of the same qualification as found in the International Court of Justice and WTO Appellate Body and where proceedings will be transparent, hearings open and comments available through EU publishing's for the public to access freely online.

Further on from the establishment of such deals as the TTIP is the plan to set up an International Investment Court to work with other countries and replace all investment dispute resolution mechanisms in existing EU agreements, EU Member States' agreements with third countries and in trade and investment treaties concluded between non-EU countries.

THE NEW DOCTRINE OF DISCOVERY

The majority of cases involving ISDS occur over natural resources of oil, gas and minerals, more over it is often related to countries trying to protect their environments, and more over again is it often always developing countries trying to protect the environment and the health and wellbeing of its people, an example of which being a recent and well known case[49] of Chevron's dumping of more than 16 billion gallons of toxic and contaminated water into the drinking water of Amazonians resulting in an Ecuadorian court ordering Chevron to pay $18 million in clean up and damages to the 30,000 indigenous. Although the decision was affirmed in 2012 in an appeals court, an ad hoc investor-state tribunal based under a U.S-Ecuador BIT (Bilateral Investment Treaty) made Ecuador not enforce the ruling, even though this treaty was established after the damage Chevron had caused.

Cases like this are numerous and if one were to research and evaluate any number the pattern would begin to emerge of what a corrupted 'free for all' the world of legal relations and negotiations has become, where parties and cases can jump territories and jurisdictions and use loop hole after loop hole to do as they wish, be it a better trade deal or escaping the payment of compensation like in the case of Chevron, even though they were at least morally obliged to.

One hope on the horizon are actions taken by the Human Rights Council in 2014 to develop 'An international legally binding instrument to regulate in international human rights law, the activities of transnational corporations and other business enterprises.'[50]

---

[49] bid., p. 2; Eduardo Garcia, 'Ecuador seeks to end investment protection treaty with U.S.', Reuters, 12 March 2013 http://uk.reuters.com/article/2013/03/12/ecuador-us-treaty idUKL1N0C401C20130312.

[50] www.southcentre.int /question/identifying-standards-for-legal-liability-of-tncs-and-other-business- enterprises-for-human-rights-violation-and-building-national-and-international-mechanisms-for-access-to- remedy/

According to the United Nations Conference on Trade and Development (UNCTD) African countries among those in the developing regions have become subject to an increasing number of ISDS cases placing even further suspicion on the rules of international investment agreements as being too open ended to interpretation and manipulation by private investment arbitrators to favour their corporate clients, deliberately inhibiting government to act in the public interest. By challenging any actions of reform they may take, in everything from alleged breaches of contract to withdrawal of previously granted subsidies and tax measures in favour of the host government.

Among case studies examined by online geopolitical studies group 'South-center[51] a number of key problems arise from how international investment agreements have been constructed as outlined in a featured article which include:

- Too much focus on investors rights and not on responsibilities.

- Little or no safeguard of the host states' regulatory authority with vague treaty provisions allowing for expansive interpretation and thus systemic bias in favour of investors asserting jurisdiction even in the face of decisions by a constitutional court of national law.

This increasing behavior by corporations through abuse of ISDS has forced several countries (developed and developing) to review their position to investment treaties and to reduce their legal liability under BITs recording a number of up to 40 as of 2012 with 60 more calling for UN intervention.

Despite such evidences of corporate behavior toward governments a recent investigation from July 2016 by Russia Today [52] typifies how they can behave just as ruthlessly, called the *War on Want's report, "The New Colonialism"* details how British Government-supported firms through a revolving door style of operations between government and industry have

---

[51] www.south.int/question/ the-rise-of-investor-state-dispute-settlement-in-the-extractive-sectors/

[52] http://tinyurl.com/zv5yhet.

gained control of Africa's energy and mineral resources, notably gold, platinum, diamonds, copper, oil, gas and coal. Up to 101 companies listed on the London stock exchange most of which being British have almost the monopoly on Africa's resources within 37 sub-Saharan African countries with an estimated value of up to $1Trillion.

The investigation also details the backing of these companies by the British Government, of both Tory and Labour Parties through the use of trade and investment policies to acquire access to Africa's resources leaving a trail of social, human and environmental abuses in its wake.

The actions and proposals of the EU and UN with newly established courts for transparency and accountability may have more positive effect on such matters, but with the tradeoff being more consolidated platforms such as the TTP for greater commercial influence over countries while forsaking national sovereignty and any semblance of existing democratic framework will certainly put the legal and political apparatus to task perhaps more than ever, only time will tell. Evidently however will it only be another vain attempt to maintain an inherently flawed system of its own design.

In closing of this section, there are two more institutions of note in the case of arbitration, being the U.S. Court of International Trade and International Court of Arbitration (ICC). In regards to the U.S (CIT) and its standing in the world, the Customs Act of 1980 as described on the website uscourts.gov is described to be 'the most significant legislation ever passed to effect international trade litigation' and 'to be the culmination of a continuous process of empiric legislation enacted over the past 200 years.' The U.S. CIT operates throughout the whole of the U.S. while also authorized to hold hearings in foreign countries. Its jurisdictional authority allows the decision of any civil action against the U.S. officers or agencies pertaining to international trade, as well as import transactions, counterclaims, cross-claims and third-party actions.

The International Court of Arbitration (ICC) based in Paris operates globally claiming to be 'the world's leading body for the resolution of the international disputes in arbitration.' Its network of global practitioners and experts place it among the leading authorities in international commercial practice. Since the 1940s the ICC has had close ties with the United Nations (UN), the World Trade Organization (WTO), the World Intellectual Property Organization (WIPO) among many other intergovernmental bodies. The ICC is also involved with global forums such as the World Summit on Sustainable Development, the UN Framework Convention on Climate Change (UNFCCC) and the Internet Governance Forum (IGF) while also having an active involvement in the WTO Expert Group on Trade Finance as well as Economic and Social Council (ECOSOC) and the International Telecommunication Union (ITU). In 2011 it was a key player in the launch of the G20 business World Trade Agenda. It also describes its global network of influence to have thousands of member companies and associates in over 130 countries with a network of national committees having 'privileged links' with major intergovernmental organizations such as the WTO.

THE LAY OF THE LAND

A 1953 film by the name of *Laxdale Hall* tells a story that could be superimposed to any place and time. It concerns a delegation of British MPs and their visit to a remote rural community in the Scottish Highlands over the matter of locals refusing to pay a road tax until the government provide better roads, with the mission in mind to impose order and collect revenues. The delegation soon upon arrival witness firsthand what they consider to be harsh and primitive living in comparison to the modern hustle and bustle of urban London, especially that of MP Samuel Pettigrew head of the delegation. A town hall meeting is organized where Pettigrew then tries to convince the community to leave their land and homes inhabited for generations to live in newly planned suburbs. When asked by a local will they have any land Pettigrew reply is no, but instead 'a modern, capitalist future, 'clean hygienic homes, profitable work and a decent standard of living... a glorious future of hard work and high wages.'

This has become the modern reality, that a majority of the ordinary populace most definitely within western territories and elsewhere throughout the world under such jurisdiction have been denied the right to own land through a complex legal and fiscal system of land division and registration that reaches back centuries in the making. The result of which being for the ordinary populace left no choice but the option to live in rented accommodation or submit to a life time of mortgage payments for a house they can call their own, when in actual fact is not nor will it ever be, even after the last payment has been made to the bank for ultimately Government has the only right of ownership.

Everything in fact registered with Government automatically gives it claim of ownership if not part ownership. Everything from your car, home, children and even marriage if registered allows them to have an authority of existence and use if given a legal reason to do so.

A fundamental legal definition to register something is to hand over legal title and thus authority and to make a public record of which, with a

Register also meaning to be a record of property and other things to be registered namely land as well as births, deaths and marriages. What makes this whole situation more of an injustice on an unsuspecting public, is that a lot of things require registration in order to live, such as having a vehicle either to travel or for a job, effectively being coercions as touched upon earlier. Such questions as how can government make us do anything and counter arguments of which will be examined in the final section of this work. For the moment it is important to clarify the role and definition of registration as the starting point in examining land ownership and the use thereof.

TORRENS AND CADASTRE

The two most historically prominent methods for both defining and disputing land ownership throughout western territories are the Torrens and Cadastre systems.

The Cadastral system was devised by the Roman Empire and conducted through public administration purely to control ownership of land by reclaiming it from private individuals while issuing taxes for usage as a further means to generate revenue by dividing up land into parcels by way of registration and included details still in use today such as ownership, tenure, location and land dimensions which would then be used to make surveys and maps.

After the fall of the Roman Empire it fell out of use in the Medieval period but found popularity again in Europe in the 16th and early 17th centuries again as a means of taxation by governments with the Napoleonic system being the modern forerunner of which is still in use particularly in the U.S. and Canada but also has a history of use throughout the west notably in the early mapping and surveying of Colonized Australia. It is used in conjunction with land title register records. Interestingly, the word also has modern etymological background as to define counties, parishes, sections, lots, blocks and city blocks.

The Torrens title is a system of land registration, named after Sir Robert Richard Torrens (1814-31) as a means to simplify land transactions and to certify the ownership of an absolute title to realty. It was common for owners needing to prove ownership of land back to the earliest grant of land by the Crown to the first owner, with documents relating to transactions with the land known as the "title deeds" or the "chain of title". Where possibly having occurred hundreds of years prior with dozens of intervening changes to land ownership a person's ownership over land could be challenged, potentially causing great legal expense to land owners and hindering any further use or development concerning the land. The system prior to Torrens was the Deeds registration system, where the instrument had registered "priority" over all instruments either unregistered or registered until afterward. The basic difference between deeds registration and the Torrens system being that the former involves registration of instruments while the latter involves registration of title, and although a register of who owned what land was maintained, it was unreliable and could be challenged in the courts at any time. This made the deeds-registration transfer of land slow, expensive, and often unable to create certain title.

The parliamentary speeches given by Torrens at the time for the adoption of his system included convincing argument for the replacement of Common law land ownership practises in the case of Australia as evidence of effect of its inadequacy in Britain to land distribution and urban planning. Property under Common law was seen to have 'sole and despotic dominion' of which Torrens argued even in their time to be an outdated and impractical while being subject to fraud and so a system was further needed for more controlled land management and use considering the particular circumstances for new colonies such as Australia and New Zealand in the 1800s.

THE HANSEATIC LEGACY

The deed system following the expansion of the U.K. Commonwealth proved inadequate due to the rise in land speculation administered through a haphazard grant system and so Torrens along with the help of a number of others particularly a German emigrant Dr juris Ulrich Hubbe from Hamburg, soon after created the system in the 1800s. The devising of the system is significant in itself and could be rightly regarded as a key event in human history and deciding point in the history of the U.K. Commonwealth, to change from Common to Commercial law in land dealings and ownership. Dr. Hü bbe was the key promoter of the German system of jurisprudence of real property law to be the adopted model, having older historical connections to the Hanseatic League [53] with aspects of Admiralty law in terms of transfer and registration provisions.

The league created the tradition of land title registration at first through public ceremony as a symbolic gesture for all to witness which over time and with the advent of writing and literacy became a recording or registration of declaration of ownership before town and city councils eventually becoming a process only done before a committee of a council. It is here perhaps the modern tradition of written record and the office and place of a register were established.

After the demise of the Hanseatic league[54] these what became City Codes were eventually replaced in the 19th Century by Civil Codes throughout German Territories of the time which included the invention of transaction real estate balance sheets for land parcels. It is here we see the Roman influence take hold by the adoption of a Civil Code system and implementation of double entry book keeping introduced to Europe by Arabic Merchants, still a basis of modern banking. In this system property

---

[53] See history of the Hanseatic league as one of the earliest pretexts to modern entrepreneurship between the twelfth and Seventeenth centuries as a private and commercial group of mercantile cities in northern Germany who had their own commercial laws, trading vessels and armies who established their own territories within the cities of countries they traded with, most notably London.

[54] A major reason for their demise being the invention of bills of exchange by Venetian bankers spread throughout Europe whereas the league traded mainly in silver coin, that and rapid changes in the geo-political landscape they were unable to compete with.

rights as assets where placed beside encumbrances as liabilities as part of registration where a certificate of title also known as a folio of register was then issued.

The Hanseatic league were noted historically also for developing their own city administrations and registrations of property at a time when the rest of Europe were still living under Monarchical and Feudal rule. Quality of life was recorded to be higher within their jurisdictions than that of Monarchs with a flourishing merchant middle class. It was the fact, that the key to the league's wealth and success lay in a monopoly on ship-building and sea trading routes as to how they developed the forerunner to modern day admiralty law by registering title to ships to be as equally important as title to land based property. The league may have had its eventual demise for a number of competing factors but as with all players studied in this essay the legal framework they devised remained and was passed down and adapted by those who came afterward, eventually to spread its influence throughout the world into the modern age.

A further influence to the German Title Registration system about the time of geo political changes in the 18th and 19th Centuries across Europe was what was known as the 'Prussian Mortgage Book' being built upon existing Hanseatic title registration frameworks saw the first combining of land title register maintained in conjunction with a cadastre system. This later influenced the British Government as well as others most notably Italy and Sweden throughout the 19th and early 20th centuries resulting in two historical pieces of legislation passed in British Parliament of the Property and Land Registration acts of 1925 giving full force of law to the Torrens system in the U.K. and its territories and basis for what has gone on to play a significant role in the development of modern mortgage and real property law in both Common and Civil jurisdictions throughout the world.[55]

In the Essay 'Torrens, Hübbe, Stewardship and the Globalisation of Property Law Systems' by Murray Raff they give further insight into aspects of the Hanseatic real property system which inspired German land law in relation to land in what is termed 'Responsible proprietorship' being a

---

[55] http://www.legislation.gov.uk/ukpga/Geo5/15-16/20/section/85

system with allocated land for specific uses such as estates for breweries, bakeries as well as residential areas and so on. Raff details how Torrens took inspiration from this in the following -

'A similar capacity was actually retained for the Torrens system by instituting an exception to the security of registered title: a paramount (overriding) interest in favour of conditions and reservations in the original Crown grant of freehold tenure - This capacity was actually utilised in the early years of the implementation of the Torrens system in Australia in order to restrict the uses to which land might be put when laying out the development of some early country towns. This was certainly done in South Australia in later periods with respect to land not under the planning authority of a local council, Reservations and conditions of the Crown grant for the benefit of mining and grazing purposes have been more common but these purposes also implement the same concept, in non-urban landscapes. In these ways, broader social intentions could be integrated in the Crown Grant with the description of the tenure.'

The Torrens system has become regarded as a major contribution to globalization in the construction of the international circulating model of land title registration by connecting the status of land title and related interests in land to cadastral information through Geographic Information Systems ('GIS') and Digital Cadastral Databases ('DCDs'). This modern implementation of technology is ongoing to attain a comparative understanding of the legal frameworks of land title registration systems employed outside Common law jurisdictions and the development of policies to accelerate the conversion of land titles remaining under the English deeds conveyance system ('the general law system') to Torrens. The system has become highly regarded and utilized also among UN mandates[56] for responsible proprietorship.

---

[56] International Conference on Land Tenure and Cadastral Infrastructure for Sustainable Development' (1999) University of Melbourne, available at <http://www. sli.unimelb.edu.au/UNConf99/index.html> at 3 October 2009.

CLAIMING THE EARTH

As tempting as it may have been to use such a sensationalist heading as Who owns the world, from a legal standpoint would be false and misleading, for even the Vatican's claim to have right of ownership to the Earth is predicated merely on the belief that the Pope is God's representative. Monarch's and Presidencies likewise claim dominion and rule over Municipalities, Principalities, Republic's, States and Commonwealths that are legal creations through Constitution and divine right both of which are founded under God .

Again if we consider the following from the Essay *'Torrens, Hubbe, Stewardship and the Globalisation of Property Law Systems'* by Murray Raff of some further points of land ownership in regards to Common law –

'The Common law idea of real property exists nowhere in pure form. The outdated common law system of real property was overturned by the comprehensive reform of real property law made by the introduction of the Torrens system. - In Common law systems one is the proprietor of the relevant abstract estate or interest in a tenure of the land, such as a fee simple estate in freehold, and not in the land itself. It would have been, and still should be possible to confine the common law presumption of 'sole and despotic dominion' to dealings with the abstract estate.'

Despite Raff focusing on the apparent Egalitarian benefits of the German Title Registration system with its notions of Responsible proprietorship they fail to address what in fact the Torrens system has since done to the detriment of ordinary people ever obtaining a right to the ownership of land well and truly, as well as there ever being a truly Egalitarian system of intelligent and prosperous land distribution, and use outside the hands of government, business and banking interests. Once again we can examine this area under the headings of Common and Civil law.

Allodial and Fee Simple may be defined by the following:

ALLODIAL: Recognizes you as the supreme owner of the land. No government can tax it and the title is passed down from parent to child or husband to wife etc. No government can trespass and no bank will ever lend money against an Allodial property because the bank has no way to foreclose against it. You have an absolute right to use lethal force to protect it.

FEE SIMPLE: Recognizes you only as a tenant on the property that you lease. The state makes the rules and trespass upon the property is allowed. The Deed can only be passed down to family members upon your death but not before your descendants open what is called an Estate in Probate, which means that the state receives a percentage of everything the decedent once owned. If you're unable to maintain payment for use of the property it can be auctioned off or a loan (mortgage) can be obtained from a bank. In a loan situation, the Deed to the property is encumbered by the bank meaning the bank is entitled to be satisfied first, if the loan (mortgage) is defaulted on for non-payment!

It must be noted however that these are general conditions under the system, despite a majority of the western body politic living under Fee Simple most countries give occupants inalienable rights within each respective Constitution under Common law, as a private property most notably a house is defined as a dwelling and cannot be entered forcefully without the permission of the owner, even by police as they take an oath to uphold the constitution of which respect and protection of family and dwellings are included. If a murder or theft were occurring inside a dwelling then anyone under common law has the right to forcefully enter the property to stop or prevent the crime, a notable side tangent is how this basic understanding is ignored or unknown to police, bailiffs and debt collectors where numerous cases can be found of the police assisting both bailiffs and debt collectors in trying to forcefully enter dwellings to seek compensation for debt payments and even physically assault occupants. Such cases as these are thankfully where Common law in the form of

Constitution still exists to protect the public. More and more cases are occurring however of Government over-ruling Constitution with Acts and Statutes eroding rights and freedoms in more and more areas of society within western countries as always for the greater good, as were led to believe. As with most subject headings explored in this work some brief historic background is useful in understanding the evolution thereof.

Fee Simple has its origins from Feudal times, the word 'fee' originally meaning 'fief' or 'Feudal' as a right in law to use the land. The Crown according to English Common law has Allodial title being the ultimate owner from which it grants estates in land,[57] hence where titles come in and the term "fee-simple title", sometimes simply "freehold". A tenant could further divide the land in to more freeholds for other tenants. There have been a number of types of fee simple for the sake of inheritance such as Fee simple absolute being the highest estate permitted by law and it gives the holder with full possessory rights and obligations now and for the future. Other fee simple estates in real property include fee simple defeasible also called fee simple determinable estates. A defeasible estate is created when a grantor places a condition on a fee simple estate in the deed, if and when a specified event happens, the estate may become void or subject to annulment.

One type of other fee simple which only seems to be practiced in the U.K is life estates used either to grant someone use of the property for the remainder of that person's life in a will, or by a grantor to reserve the right to continue using the property for the remainder of the grantor's life after it is sold. The right to ownership of the property after the death of the life estate owner is called the remainder estate but is conducted under the terms of equity and not as a right in property while the grantor is alive.

---

[57] Before the year 1066 the people of England held Allodial title to their land. Not even the king could take the land for not paying a tithe. William the Conquer came in 1066 and stole the Kings Title and took the land of the people. From William I, 1066, to King John, 1199, England was in dire straits and bankrupt. John enacted Mortmain to acquire real property taxes as will be detailed beginning on page 115.

As stated in the above definition of fee simple many jurisdictions have created financial obligations that may be imposed on a freehold estate, such examples being an estate tax in the U.K and a property tax in the U.S.

Where fee simple is an estate in land, Allodial constitutes ownership of real property being land, buildings and fixtures with no superior lord, and where only Monarchs and Governments as hinted above with the English Crown have ever had superior and absolute ownership of. Allodial title is related to the concept of land held "in allodium" or land ownership by occupancy and defence of that land.

Historically, much of land was uninhabited and could therefore be held "in allodium". The U.S. and U.K. with its Commonwealth particularly of Western territories operate by eminent domain, being the right of government or its agents to expropriate private property for public use with payment of compensation. In the UK it is used chiefly through International Law, whereas in the U.S through Federal and State governments. Outside of certain historical events such as the Aboriginals of Australia and Maori of New Zealand being granted rights to own territories when the Colonization of these countries first occurred. No other Commonwealth territories and citizens therein have rights to Allodial title.

In the case of civil law territories such as France Allodial title only existed before the French Revolution with ecclesiastical properties and property fallen out of feudal ownership to have title. After the French Revolution it became the norm in France and other civil law countries under Napoleonic legal influence. In October, 1854, the Seigneurial system of Lower Canada ceded from France to Britain in 1763 after 'the Seven Years' War, was replaced by the Seigneurial[58] Tenures Abolition Act of October 1854, and a form similar to a Socage system59 replaced it. Allodial title also has origins in Northern Germany from the Salic law system which lasted from A.D 507-596 being common throughout northern Europe, but now relatively unknown to

---

[58] A term for a feudal lord.

[59] A feudal tenure of land involving payment of rent or other non-military service to a superior.

common law jurisdictions apart from the U.S.[60] Other last remaining areas of Allodial titles in the west are known as feudal tenure in the U.K. territories of Orkney and Shetland.

---

[60] Nevada and Texas have provisions for considering land Allodial under state law.

THE TUDOR PERIOD & THE LAND REGISTRY

To avoid estate taxes in England owners found a legal loophole in wiling it to a trustee for the use of them being the beneficiary. The Common law courts refused to recognize this clause instead granting title to the trustee. Courts of equity were developed and established jurisdiction over the matter to avoid having the trustee taking title from the owner and instead make the trustee an owner in equity, being only the use of the land. The outcome from this historically led to the establishment of what has become the mortgage and security process. Enjoyment of the property during the period where the mortgage was in good standing could be assured through the equity courts, while the right to foreclose on the property to merge the common law and equity title were guaranteed in the common law courts, which is still the case today.

As previously examined, before the introduction of the Torrens system real property and proof of title was conducted by the Deeds registration system through title deeds and chain of title. With the Torrens system came the establishment of the land registry where a central office was responsible for the filing of land deeds, mortgages, liens and other evidence of ownership, as well as transfer or encumbrance. Under land registry, deeds and charges were not recognized unless they filed, and those who filed were given priority over previous transactions not been filed. Moreover, under statutes of limitation certain jurisdictions only accepted documents being filed 40 years previous, which had to then be consulted to determine chain of ownership. This has since been implemented and established across U.K. Commonwealth territories and maintained thereafter under statute beginning with such events as the Property and Land Registration acts of 1925, with the events of the 1930s tying in shortly thereafter with equity, securities and mortgages being among the instruments used in the global domination of a debt and credit based banking system as exist today, alongside the frameworks of property and commercial code practices in both traditionally civil and common law territories as examined earlier.

In the case of the U.S. the Treaty of Paris in 1783 as well as recognizing American independence coincidently ended any residual rights held by the Crown, where all land in the American colonies given by royal grants conducted under fee simple owed any allegiance or duty to the Crown with no specific reference to Allodial title in the text of the treaty. Some states as historically noted created a form of Allodial title while others retained the Tenurial system with the state as the new ultimate landholder. Essentially states and their territories formed by purchase, treaty or annexation.

Many state constitutions such as Arkansas, Wisconsin, Minnesota and New York refer to Allodial title, but only to be distinguished from feudal title. Government however can compel the sale of privately owned real property for public necessity by eminent domain laws in both federal and state government. Additional features to the U.S. framework are that the Fifth Amendment requires just compensation for eminent domain compelled sales. As well that government powers of policing and escheat[61] have been retained in the American legal system.

Any last vestiges of states being sovereign was diminished after the bankruptcy of the U.S. in 1933 of which strong evidence postulates the entire continent was acquired by creditors (banking elite) through escheat and turned into a truly commercial operation thereafter as with the rest of the west.

---

[61] The reversion of property to the state, or (in feudal law) to a lord, on the owner's dying without legal heirs.

ORIGINS OF ESCHEAT

The issue of escheat seems to be a universal aspect across western territories, which by no surprise has its origins in Rome and again later with the events of 1213-15 A.D. with King James of England and Pope Innocent III.

The infamous story of Nero and the great fire of Rome many researchers postulate to have had a manipulative hidden legal motive behind the popular tale of the alleged mad emperor. In the aftermath of the great fire Nero had the Senate create a land Trust to include all the estates of Rome which then Nero proclaimed all owners to be legally dead appointing the senate as Trustees to acquire a percentage of crops and to issue excessive taxes to its heirs, as well as in case of the owner having actually died and without a last will and testament the estate would then become sold to a member of the senate.

Nero used the ignorance of the citizenry in legal matters of how to reclaim their property and fear of punishment for challenging his word as Emperor so as to have no choice but to remain in servitude. The Vatican would continue such practices in the centuries to follow thriving on superstition, fear and ignorance of the masses. This same fear and ignorance in dealing with perceived authority is self-evident to this day.

One other historically notable example of this legal ploy in the creation of a legal trust comes from the great fire of London in 1666 where identical tactics in the acquiring of land and real estate of the greater area now commonly known as the City-State of London occurred. We will now take a closer look at the events of the significance of the Magna Carta of 1213 A.D.

MORTMAIN AND THE MAGNA CARTA

The outcome of the 1213 A.D. treaty between King James of England and Pope Innocent III as touched upon earlier is historically revered as one of the major events in western legal history, and here's how.

As previously mentioned James had signed the Magna Carta fearing a rebellion, by signing the Magna Cart James effectively set all Dukes, Lords and Nobles with land granted by the Crown on equal footing with him and the Pope making them sovereign, this prevented the return of their estates to the king upon their death, hence having Allodial title. James cleverly invoked the ancient law of Mortmain ('The dead man's hand') establishing the basis of modern day legal probate with a percentage of tax of a deceased estate being paid to the Crown, (not unlike the legal trick of Nero) further still, upon distribution of a dead person's estate and failure to pay this tax ownership of the estate was sold by the court to pay the tax and absent a valid last will and testament the estate was returned to the Crown. A modern comparison of this being a return of estate to the Federal Government or respective State in the U.S.

By signing the Magna Carta and enacting Mortmain made Pope Innocent III furious as for placing others on equal footing with the King and he, and that Mortmain prevented Catholic Parishioners in the willing of deeds and land to the Church and further obligating the Church to pay the Kings probate tax. The Pope immediately declared the Magna Carta an unlawful affront to the Church and its rule. This then led to an act of contrition by John to regain favour. Among the concessions they had to make where, that all land titles of England, Ireland and France belonged to the Church, as well as all land and oceans of the earth and that John recognise the Pope as the Vicar of Christ by Royal Decree.

The late John Harris (1964-2015) a U.K. legal researcher and lecturer in an article featured on the website they founded TPUC.org titled The slavery foundation stone and deception of the Magna Carta give their opinion on these events which help give strong clue to the significance of the Pope and Church in the development of modern 'democracy' and its influence on the

English Monarchy as relevant to the rest of the western world throughout history beginning from the events of 1213 A.D.[62]

Harris postulated that the Papacy now having put King John into a binding contract with risk of excommunication needed a way to maintain it through his heirs and successors and did so through the Dukes, Lords and Nobles being made to rebel and so actually had John sign the Magna Carta under the influence of the Archbishop of Canterbury among others who were historically recorded to be at the signing as a smoke screen, as the Pope knew the Dukes, Lords and Nobles were needed to keep John in line, and so Harris further postulates that they were appeased in return for their loyalty by greed, power and position as well as a council and later parliament being created consisting largely of clergy to keep close to the Monarchy which later over successive centuries and decades came to form the English Parliament in its modern form of which the powerful and influential entities of the Crown Temple along with the Banking and Judicial system of the City of London grew up alongside. Indeed, the evidence is strong in such sequence of events that the Monarch aristocrats of England have not been ruling sovereigns since the reign of King John's treaty with the outcomes signing the Magna Carta and treaty thereafter with the Papacy.

All royal sovereignty of the old British Crown since which time have passed to the Crown Temple in Chancery. Successive constitutions such as the Magna Carta of 1297, the Provisions of Oxford and Provisions of Westminster were key events in the formation of Parliament having power over the Monarchy and prevalence of Common Law over Absolute Monarchical rule, with the eventual formation of Constitutional Monarchy today with the Bill of Rights of 1688, the Act of Settlement of 1701, and the Act of Union 1706 with the Monarch now being appointed by Parliament. The Queen is a 'Statutory Monarch' and has no powers separate from the UK Parliament with no legal power to make decisions and only endorse and/or carry out decisions made by the Ministers that appointed her. Furthermore,

---

[62] The Norman invasion of the 11th century of England which included the Popes blessing could officially be said to be the start of such events but the 13th century being when the Papacy made the bold move to rule England from affair.

the monarch has not executive function within the Commonwealth with the role now being made purely titular. [63]

Concerning the 1213 Magna Carta however, Harris further argued was in fact a legal instrument (contract) to secure the longevity of the English monarchy's allegiance to the papacy and the foundation for the administration of Canon law in the U.K and its territories conducted through a parliament while being taken to mistakenly represent an historical foundation for democratic governance as has occurred in popular history, for as Harris explains to the legally illiterate to represent anything but, as often being called one of the great charters of liberty, liberty for who exactly is the question. As Harris points out the legal definition of a charter to be -

'Charter: A written grant from the sovereign power of a country conferring certain rights and privileges on a person or a corporation, also: A document incorporating an institution and specifying its rights; includes the articles of incorporation and the certificate of incorporation.'

Thereafter giving appropriate legal definition and terms to the wording therein -

'As you can see a charter is a grant that does not apply to men, women and children it applies to 'persons', as long as you are deemed as to have the 'privileges of a person'. Under canon law although man and person are synonymous in grammar, not all men were classed as persons as slaves were classed as 'things'. At this time in England most of us would have been serfs; in other words, slaves and this would have been the majority of us, so to any lord we would have been things and things (chattels) have no rights. They have no personality they are personality: moveable property and Williams 'Doomsday Book' was a list of all his personality, as all censuses are..'

They further give appropriate legal definition and clarification of the word liberty aside from the general English definition to include the condition of being physically and legally free from confinement, servitude, forced labour, privileges, rights etc civil liberties, they explain -

---

[63] Holding or constituting a purely formal position or title without any real authority.

'Something that is plainly obvious starts to emerge. As it says above legally free, but 'things' cannot be legally free as they have no legal personality i.e. 'status' they do not exist in the legal world, so in effect they have no legal rights. 'Things' are not physically or legally free and can be kept in confinement, servitude under forced labour, they have no privileges, or rights and no civil liberties. 'Things' do not enjoy social, political or economic rights and privileges, they are property of another under the whim of that other. Liberty is not freedom, liberty is a grant of rights, but would only apply to the ones of status, those who believed they were better in some way, as we would know it now the upper class high society.'

In the following Harris gives an excellent summation of the persisting conditions of the legal reality with further regards to liberty regardless of time, place or history -

'The concept of liberty forms the core of all democratic principles and societies, yet as a legal concept it defies clear definition, which to me is very obvious because it actually defines slavery and is the antithesis of moral or natural as slavery is. We must remember that legal is in form only (persons) a category of 'things' distinguished by some common characteristic or quality and within this comes the legal ability to enslave those of lesser quality. '

Saying further -

'A master slave syndrome maintained by an immoral legal concept in the form of liberty under a false belief system based upon nothing more than human suffering and a delusional miscomprehension that anything and everything is ok, as long as it has the label 'legal' upon it such as war. '

Harris also stated that they believed the Magna Carta was a first western document of its kind to make laws of oppression legal in which case, and being the first of many to pave the way for many further legal devises to keep the English Monarchy in check for generations to come in binding them to legal doctrine dictated by the Roman Papacy's system of Canon/Civil law issued throughout western Monarchs and Parliaments in time and with the advent of discovering new lands and the importance of vessels and trade added that of Admiralty and Commercial law to its framework eventually leading to the modern age and legal reality as it stands.

BREAKING CONTRACT WITH ROME

The notorious events of the Tudor Monarch Henry VIII breaking with the Papacy for not annulling a marriage seem to draw the line in history of its power and influence in England through the Act in Restraint of Annates in 1532 removing Papal authority in England and Wales, as Annates [64] were the main source of income in Rome from England and this act all but banned this practice. Henry suspended it initially as to put pressure on the Papacy to give him his annulment. Only when it became clear it wouldn't be granted was it introduced into law. This was followed by the Act in Restraints of Appeals in 1533 removing full legal and canonical powers from the Church to Government and the Monarch with the final declaration of removal of Papal authority from England with the Act Extinguishing the Authority of the Bishop in Rome in 1536.

As noted earlier all lands in France as well as throughout a majority of western Europe remained under Feudal (fee simple) rule except property of the Church until Napoleon historically diminished territorial dominance of the Church in the 1800s [65] and weakening its political influence.[66] While even after its come back and the demise of Napoleon set it on a road to modernity through the historical events deciding its territorial and political influence of Italian Unification period between 1871 and 1918 with the establishment of the Kingdom of Italy and the Lantern Treaty of 1929 during the Dictatorship of Mussolini.

---

[64] A year's revenue of a Roman Catholic see or benefice, paid to the Pope by a bishop or other cleric on his appointment.

[65] Napoleon even went so far as to remove the entire Vatican secret library to Paris while sacking the Vatican in 1809 later taking the Vatican three years to return to Rome.

[66] The law of the Civil Constitution of the Clergy of 1790 declared there was to be just one bishop for each Department, and in a radical move to democratize the church, the Bishop, like the priests, was to be elected by the people. Furthermore, all clergy were to swear allegiance to the state and king above the Pope.

THE AGE OF COMMERCE

An underlying theme throughout this work has been to demonstrate just how the legal framework remains and continues throughout, despite whoever are in power and whenever that may be appears to make no difference, as figureheads come and go but ideas remain as self-evident of the Vatican, Popes, Monarchs and Government.

The dawn of the twentieth century has seen the demise and irrelevance of the old rule of figureheads and the rise of the financial and legal frameworks of power and control such as through trade partnerships and agreements, central banks conducted from the political, financial, legal, militaristic and religious hubs of the City of London, Washington D.C and the Vatican as well the Bank of International Settlements in Switzerland.

The British Crown has long been transferred to being a major corporate entity, the Vatican has established itself in the modern age by quietly controlling interests in construction, utilities, manufacturing, real estate and financial operations the length and breadth of Italy and to a considerable degree throughout Europe and the world. Besides its obvious Religious status its diplomatic and tax exempt conditions of status remain as considerable factors in its longevity and power also among other religions and institutions of global influence.

While the growing reality of the increasing majority of the governments of both developed and developing countries across the world having taken up corporate status or in the process of doing so all the while privatising and auctioneering the natural resources, utilities and services of their territories, unbeknownst to the tax paying majority of their citizenry, violating their constitutional oaths and duties to both citizen and country in the process.[67] Before concluding this section, it is worth taking a look at those across the globe with the most Allodial and Fee Simple right to land.

---

[67] As an example George Bush.Snr signed off Executive Order 12803 - Infrastructure Privatization on April 30, 1992 privatizing the United States of America to be sold off piece by piece to any and all private commercial interests.

KEEPING BOUNDARIES

A fact perhaps known among NLRBE advocators worldwide and to all readers otherwise of the root cause of poverty and material inequality stems directly from access to land distribution and utilisation, and therefore resources. The key events and legal means as covered previously is hoped have provided ample clarification of why this remains to be. The acquisition of land either by violent or legal means is the very basis of socioeconomic history; without land nothing else would be possible. Indeed we are still living in the past and situations not appearing to be any more progressive with all manner of events of people being harassed or even arrested, such as from growing food in their gardens to collecting rain water on the properties they occupy. Once again were seeing an ignorance of lawful and legal conduct among both the public and alleged authorities.

An article featured in the magazine New Statesman by Author Kevin Cahill whose book *Who Owns the World: The Hidden Facts Behind Landownership* details some interesting figures, which they give to be -

"The world relative to its human population is quite large. It is 123 billion acres in size, of which 37 billion acres are land. This means that there are a notional four acres available for every man, woman and child in the predicted 2050 world population Of nine billion, which would be an increase of two billion on the present population. But notional is not real, and what is noticeable when looking at how the 37 billion acres are used by nature and humanity is that the urban area, humanity's footprint on the land patch, is extremely small, at 1.5 per cent. This conflicts with the common rhetoric of environmentalists, which too often comes fact-free."

Cahill quickly moves into discussing land ownership, of the differences related to land ownership type related to economic health and where countries such as the United States, Germany and France in the practice of allowing private ownership fair better than feudal or Monarchical based territories with the U.K. Commonwealth being perhaps the most notable exception with Great Britain, Australia, New Zealand and Canada and where the Crown with Queen Elizabeth as head of State is by far the biggest (feudal) land title owner on the planet with 32 countries, a Commonwealth of 54 countries that contain a quarter of the world's population while being legal owner of an estimated 6.6 billion acres; one-sixth of the earth's non-ocean surface.

Cahill makes the correct line of inquiry by delving further back in history of the Roman influence to the attitude and practice of land acquisition, ownership and use having been brought to England in 43 A.D. and later again with the noted influence of the Norman Invasion of 1066 before then mentioning the taking and exercising of these legal practices across the world with the British Empire. Outside of the Commonwealth, Cahill notes the Chinese totalitarian government and Russian Government to be the next largest state owners and individual landowner monarch to be the King of Saudi Arabia.

Also noted is the commonality of a number of other monarchs around the world to rule effectively as 'Trustees to God' of the land which include the King of Morocco, Sultan Quaboos of Oman, King Abdullah of Jordan, the Emir of Kuwait and Sheikh Hamad of Qatar. Not forgetting the Pope of course having nearly as many acres as the Crown, estimated at one time to be between 20 and 30 per cent of Europe and a same proportion of South America according to Cahill's research though having been lost over time, but the Church's worldwide institutions, religious orders and dioceses are estimated at a total of 177 million acres of which the Pope is the sole owner. Outside of non-monarchical, non-state and non-church landholdings are a number of private landholders[68] of which Cahill mentions most notably to be American Ted Turner.

---

[68] http://www.therichest.com/rich-list/the-biggest/12-of-the-biggest-land-owners-on-earth/

LAND, ECONOMY AND POPULATION

In terms of economic activity in relation to population and land size ratios, Cahill makes the comparison of among the two most prominent developed countries in terms of their landmass being the U.S. and Australia, making the point of how Australia demonstrates how a small population can create huge landholdings if plentiful in comparison to the size of America having a relatively large population in relation to land availability, particularly for agricultural use. As well how both countries practice free-market capitalism, with the American model based mainly on industry and population, while Australia is based on a combination of agriculture and mined minerals, also with Australia demonstrating economic prosperity at a corporate level is possible when not formally impeded by feudal structures to operate. The dominant worldwide trend of movement of people from rural to urban areas of which Cahill takes note, having first began in 18th century Europe is now taking place worldwide most notably in Africa, Asia and the middle east toward the west, driven overwhelmingly by the factors of poverty, war and natural disasters.

Further from this do they pose the question of the rise of technical unemployment in the last fifty years and what will become of populations in developed and developing regions alike across the world, to which they see a base solution for such future uncertainties to be the necessary change in nature and attitude to land ownership, as well to address the current flaws and falsehoods of Infinite economic growth, Capitalism and taxation inequality. One final comment is made of addressing the issue of over population, which they again say lies in redefining land access and distribution as key to future human prosperity.

TAKING LEAVE OF OUR CENSUS

One final but important subject to conclude on this particular section is that of Government Census. The origins of which, again to no surprise stem from the Roman Empire in the registering of citizens and property for the purposes of taxation.

These forms of data collection on the body politic, which depending on its whereabouts can be every four to five or ten years, even being as often as every year have more and more become an encroachment on rights to privacy with a threat of being fined or imprisonment in some western countries for non- compliance. Although it may not be something often on the minds of the public due to being only every number of years, proves a perfect example of what others refer to as 'totalitarian tip toe'. The latest example from Australia has seen major public backlash even from some within government[69] for making names and addresses mandatory to be kept for up to ten years, on top which experiencing the latest of a string of hacks for the Australian Bureau of Statistics (ABS) resulting in a disastrously unpopular 2016 Census suffering national and international embarrassment and governmental distrust. The public took to online social media to vent their frustrations as well with online media posting articles citing legal loopholes[70] as well with legal and census experts explaining how to legally leave your name off of the submitted form, while other bodies calling for the census to be scraped and government fear mongering of fines to be removed permanently. [71]

Other criticisms can be found with other countries making it mandatory with risk of penalty for non-compliance such as Ireland, Canada and the U.S. In Ireland's case a ludicrously large fee was threatened for non-compliance of EUR 44,000 for the 2016 Census with some legal researchers there argue the Census to be unconstitutional as violating the right to privacy within the family unit and thus the family dwelling, although a few cases

---

[69] http://www.abc.net.au/news/2016-08-08/nick-xenophon-to-withhold-name-in-census-over-privacy-concerns/7702304

[70] https://www.crikey.com.au/2016/07/14/census-cannot-force-you-to-give-data/

[71] https://www.privacy.org.au/Media/MR-Census-160810.pdf

were reported in the national media in 2011 for non-compliance those summoned to court were not charged the non-compliance amount with one case winning on constitutional grounds.

The Canadian government have threatened imprisonment for non-compliance by the present government in power wanting to make the Census mandatory after recently bringing it back[72]. The U.S. Federal Government have a Census in some parts of the country nearly every year with a nationwide Census every 10 years.

Legal and financial researcher Jerry Day has produced an excellent and informative two-part video series[73] concerning the subject of government issued Census in the case of the U.S, debunking and rebutting many of the claims for its extreme invasion of privacy in most cases on Constitutional grounds. An excellent criticism and summation of Census privacy invasion in the face of government rhetoric claiming to be for better distribution of Federal benefits and resources, they give in the following –

> "To my knowledge the government distribute benefits by ear marks and political expediency in areas where it wishes to gain influence and most distributions are no longer discretionary, most revenues are committed to prior obligations, any further obligations are funded one hundred percent by debt. Census data is far more likely to be used for the targeted generation of taxes, licences, fees, fines and other forms of wealth extraction than they are to be used for wealth distribution."

---

[72] Will Canadians who refuse to complete long-form census go to jail? https://www.youtube.com/watch?v=qkYgb3_OSCw

[73] The Census is getting personal https://www.youtube.com/watch?v=RsDhkPym01k Census Video Part2, Clarifications https://www.youtube.com/watch?v=LFvS5m4_OtA

THE KINGDOM OF IDEAS

Of all the case history featured throughout this work thus far, a fitting bookend to this section comes from Australian legal researcher Santos Bonnaci summarizing perfectly the underlying theme of the long lasting influence of the Roman Empire self-evident throughout this work where having once said -

> 'For thousands of years Rome has been making slaves and fools of mankind! The time has come to be free forever from the inventions of the most powerful empire the world has ever known. The inventions of the Kingdom of ideas that is Rome, are The Julio/ Gregorian Calendar, the Latin Language, Capitalism, Fictional Christianity, Democracy, Cannon Law (Maritime Law), Phoney Money (Fiat currency, interest laden Money) and the Corporation.
>
> All of the above are fictional creations through which Rome has subjugated the whole inhabited Earth. Imperialism is the order of the day, land grabbing, inquisitions, crusades, medicating the masses, Industrial Military Complex, inflation, constant wars. All these are the services that Rome has to offer. '

SECTION TWO
THE CIRCUMSTANCE

To recall the analogy of the quote as taken from the Impressionist painter Pissaro, having now finished with the broom can we now move on to the needle. With the map of history having been examined and stories refreshed in our minds we now move forward to the finer details of the moment, of that which keeps the legal reality alive and humanity enslaved. Building on what we know of the global socioeconomic changes that occurred in the 1930s, Government and indeed the world would never be the same again.

The following presents a recent case study of the Australian government as one of the most researched and verified examples of how Government, most certainly in the west, has become fully corporatized and operate merely as de facto for profit entities on an unsuspecting public and not de jure government founded upon constitution under God, and as the evidence will show having further become party to man-made covenants of the League of Nations and later the United Nations creating a further questioning of status and validity, and thus knowingly perpetuating the continuation of the greatest fraud in history, of the global legal reality itself.

QUESTIONING GOVERNMENT
AUSTRALIA – A CASE STUDY

The research and educational efforts of two Australians; active researcher and activist Scott Bartle and a former researcher and activist by the Alias of Thomas Anderson have both helped tremendously in exposing the Australian government and its fiscal/Commercial operations, both of whom came to their conclusions for very different reasons but have the commonality of indeed having done a service to humanity in helping to shed more light on the fraud of the global legal reality at play holding humanity in its grip perpetuated on a daily basis. By simply asking these alleged authorities to present their proof of claim of that authority while in the process exposing the flaws in the fraud of their operations.

What began as a routine matter for West Australian Scott Bartle in being ordered to pay excess taxes for importing a car from the U.S. into Australia led to the discovery of perhaps the biggest smoking gun in the country's history if not that of government in the twentieth century, having uncovered if not rediscovered some forgotten truths about the historical foundations of Australian government.[74] By refusing to pay what they felt was an unjust tax Scott decided to challenge the authorities in customs on the matter through notice. After Scott's research led to discovering that the Australian Government was registered as a company with the SEC (Securities and Exchange Commission) of Washington D.C and the Coat of Arms of the Australian government being a registered trademark with the U.S. Patent and Trademark office drew further suspicion leading to question the validity of the Australian Government in general.

---

[74] www.truth-now.net

WHICH GOVERNMENT, WHICH PARLIAMENT, WHICH QUEEN?

By referring back to the Commonwealth of Australia Constitution Act of 1900 Scott first noticed government was named to be Government of the Commonwealth of Australia which today is Australian Government same as when referencing Parliament in the 1900 Act being Parliament of the Commonwealth now called Parliament of Australia. Scott found no record of referendum for when this name changed occurred being mandatory under Section 128 Clause 9 of the Act regarding alterations to the Constitution. Also was the matter of Queen Elizabeth II being the Heir and Successor to Queen Victoria signatory of the Letters Patent of the 1900 Act giving its power and validity. Scott found current references of the Queen to be 'Queen of Australia', which if we recall, the U.K Monarchy having only statutory power can only endorse decisions made by parliament, furthermore the title of 'Queen of Australia' is merely a titular title holding no legal power whatsoever. Additional historic evidence shows that Elizabeth with no authority of the U.K Parliament signed the Royal Styles and Titles Act 1973 repealing the previous Royals Styles and Titles Act of 1953 creating the office of Queen of Australia however even if were valid a referendum would be required to adopt which never took place.

Scott also found the office of Governor-General which according to the 1900 Act is the Commander-in-Chief of the Commonwealth of Australia for the heirs and Successors of Queen Victoria to be holding the office and title under the 'Queen of Australia' and the 'Seal of Australia' and likewise who's oath is meant to be prescribed under the same Letters Patent as per the 1900 Act, Scott found to be made under the 'Seal of Australia' in front of the Chief Justice of the Supreme Court of whatever state they maybe in, such as Western Australia.

Addition to this Scott researched other key important figures in government such as Senators who are supposed to be certified by a properly appointed Governor-General as Parliament of the Commonwealth, found instead Senators to be certified by State Governors as well the Chief Justice of the High Court of Australia as defined within the 1900 Act, found there to be a Chief Justice of Australia without valid Commission or witnesses present in the taking of the Governor General's Oaths, with the office of Justices likewise meant to be constituted and appointed by the Governor of a state under the Great Seal of the U.K. found to be appointed by the Governor under the Great Seal of the Australian Government, a proven trade mark and not one of Monarchical power.

THE AUSTRALIAN CONSTITUTIONAL QUAGMIRE

To recall the analogy as mentioned previous pertaining to governance and the hierarchy of law, Divine law/Gods law being the highest under which constitutions and Ecclesiastical /Canon law are founded. These evidences of alleged de- jure/Common law Government behaving and operating as de facto/ corporate entities completely destroys their validity as government of nations and the issuer of laws of socioeconomic conduct no more than any other corporate entity outside of such things as employee policies, it is just like the fiat money system, a faith and confidence trick on an unsuspecting and uneducated public.

The history of the formation of the Australian government and constitution make an ideal case study due to the number of questionable historic and legal episodes that take into account Scott Bartle's justified scepticisms being too crucial to ignore, and demonstrate the abuses having been made by those in power as further proof of the fact that the legal reality is perpetuated as a means to control and deceive the masses and to maintain wealth/ rule divide.

The validity for the basis of Australian government is marred in a history of legal and diplomatic double standard continuing to this day, having had several occasions for its status verified which include:

- The Commonwealth of Australia Act 1900.

- The signing of and unanimous vote by the Federal Parliament of the Commonwealth of Australia in acceptance of the Treaty of Versailles in 1919.

- The declaration of the Inter-Imperial Relations Committee of the Imperial Conference. 1929 by the Balfour Declaration

- The Federal Parliament of the Commonwealth of Australia enacting the Statute of Westminster Adoption Act 1942 back dated to 1939.
- the Commonwealth of Australia becoming a foundation member of the United Nations and subsequently enacting the Charter of the Unite Nations Act 1945.

- The 1986 with the passing of the Australia and U.K Acts.

The rub, so to speak, of this history can be summarized as follows: The Australian Government cannot rely upon any body of law from the U.K upon becoming a sovereign nation in the eyes of International law with the Treaty of Versailles, and thereafter in 1920 becoming a member in the League of Nations, again being reconfirmed in 1945 as a member of the UN in that regard, and yet still relies on the Commonwealth of Australia Act 1900 for its legal basis clearly breaching International law. The Australian people do not even have ultimate control over the 'Australian' Constitution. In 1995 the Lord Chancellor of the UK in answer to a Parliamentary question asked in the UK Parliament about the Australian Constitution, stated:

> "The British Constitution Act 1900 was for self-government. It was never intended to be and is not suitable to be the basis for independence. The right to repeal this Act remains the sole prerogative of the United Kingdom. There is no means by which under United Kingdom or international law. This power can be transferred to a foreign country or Member State of the United Nations. Indeed, the United Nations Charter precludes any such action".

LOCAL "GOVERNMENT"

As of 1919 the Act of 1900 became ultra vires [75] yet it continues to be used by the Australian Government for the maintaining of parliament and all government branches such as the tax office while denying Australian citizens inalienable rights to self-determination let alone the subject of local councils in Australia who behave as a law onto themselves while ignoring Federal law as they introduce more levies and taxes annually and give themselves pay rises and continually prohibit or ignore questions from the public they supposedly represent often exposing them as opportunists.[76]

These Local Councils are essentially unlawful and illegal entities operating with impunity based solely on the assumption of Federal Government ignoring the Constitution. The revenue made by local councils are in the form of land tax (rates), permits, fee's, fines etc, even though the people of Australia have twice said no in referendums to their very existence. Under the Constitution in place in Australia supporting an unlawful entity is still considered a crime. Local Councils are not local Government as there is no such a thing. Those in power at the state and local levels across Australia have tried three times since the 1970s to gain these entities Constitutional recognition to solidify their power of place indefinitely as a sign of such corruption, as any such entity claiming to be local government is unlawful as they are not public/government owned entities and are corporate entities many of which owned by foreign interests being allowed to continually extort an unknowing and ignorant public. Many cases with them issuing rates/land tax notices and other requests across the country are again unknown to the general public are unlawful, as only the Federal Government can raise a tax on the people with State governments forbidden from raising taxes. Local Council land tax (rates) violate the agreement under title of all land held in Australia under fee simple.

---

[75] Beyond one's legal power or authority
[76] Search for 'Pirates of the suburbs' on youtube

The State Governments of Australia created the LGA (Local Government Act) - this act substantially changed all State constitutions and gave more power to the government and as such under all State and federal law it should have been put to the people for approval at a State referendum - this never occurred making the LGA totally unlawful. Under the law and many human rights agreements to which Australia is a signatory this is not only unlawful and a violation of international human rights but rightly considered slavery under the act in the form of involuntary debt. This is certainly an issue for further investigation across the world of all jurisdictions in questioning the validity of federal and local so called government.

THE LEGAL VOID

Since 1919 the historical evidence thereafter showed clearly the cover-ups needed to bridge the legal void left in place in the creation of a political and judicial system and the change in sovereignty for Australia. All Judicial offices from the Governor-General, State and Territory Governors, parliamentarians and Senators and all other involved parties such as the Police are technically operating as U.K agents.

Also, astonishingly and quite heinously the Australian Government adopted the Statute of Westminster 1931 (UK) in 1942 retroactively commencing it from the 3rd September 1939 as a legal step to rule out any illegality of involvement in WWII by not having formally declared war on Germany 3 years earlier as the Statute was adopted about the time war was declared on Japan and the Australian Parliament needed to be sure of its power to do so.

In an attempt to make links between the original Act of 1900, in 1984 an Act called The Letters Patent Relating to her Office of Governor-General of the Commonwealth of Australia as a continuation of the original terms of the 1900 Act, being that Queen Victoria having died in 1900 left no Letters Patent and so as to be a clause for any 'invalid' Commission or appointment made thereafter to be legally authorized.

The Australia Act of 1986 followed having two Acts, one from either country but were not registered as required under the Charter of the United Nations to have extra-territorial effect, and consequently cannot be relied on in any international forum.

Notwithstanding the international status of the Act it still ensured British colonial law was to continue in Australia. Despite including sections to say otherwise being subject to interpretation, as with all things law. The Act really didn't remove British law used in Australia but only referred to new British law at the time, as Australian Commonwealth State Statute books are still based upon British law as well as Australian courts. Also Australia continues to have a monarch who derives her power from the British Parliament, and she remains the Executive Head of Government of the six Australian States. So to exercise her power in those States, her power must be seen as an extension of power of the UK Parliament. As well being that the new letters Patent were written drafted and executed by the Chancellors Office in the UK Parliament not a Governor-General of Australia.

All laws pertaining to state territories are then likewise brought to question, all contracts, peace treaties, trade negotiations and defense alliances made with other countries as well as intellectual property and patents. There is also the issue of Australian Citizens having access to the same rights as British Citizens such as the European Convention of Human Rights and Fundamental freedoms, seeing that the Australian high court has declared that Australia is governed under British domestic legislation. This also puts into question other issues such as the validity of Citizenship granted to foreigners.

INTERNATIONAL CONCERN

Although not something often to be in the media spotlight this history of legal disarray for Australia has indeed been brought to the attention of Prime Ministers, Attorney-Generals and other Senior Cabinet Ministers and party leaders within the walls of Canberra along with documents being presented in many a court case both in and outside of Australia highlighting the issue.[77] While also being brought to the attention of all 185 Member States of the United Nations as well as to Kofi Annan the General Secretariat, the Human Rights Commission, the Human Rights Committee and the Security Council. A main issue of the document concerns the establishment of an International Criminal Tribunal for the inhibition of inalienable rights to Australian citizens of self-determination by those in power knowingly subjecting Australian citizens to British colonial law within the sovereign territory of the Commonwealth of Australia.

The media as well as legal, academic and political communities will certainly need to be among those to address the issue and bring into the open for further questioning. As to general public perception, a notable example being in November of 1999 when the people of Australia by referendum had for the first time the opportunity to have their say regarding the acceptance or otherwise of the Constitution under which they are governed. The proposition was rejected in every State and Territory of Australia on a national basis of 60.66% to 39.34%. Notably this was about the same time the issue came to the conscience of government with it being 53 years since Australia was recognized as a sovereign by both the U.N and U.K, strongly suggesting the coinciding of the referendum.

The maintaining of the 'order of things' by the Australian establishment as far as this section has been able to cover, an educated guess would be to conclude obviously for fiscal advantage in maintaining the legal framework to the detriment of the citizenry.

---

[77] Time constraints did not allow for the research of cases.

This quagmire of a double legitimate standard being entertained atop the corporate nature the Australian government among many others stand as valid proof of how the law and money makers, and status quo keepers will go to any lengths to bend and break their own rules to ensure institutional preservation for apparent benevolent means, even if to bring about malevolent consequence.

TAXES
The Australian ATO - a case study

Of all issues of contention in dealing with government among the highest most certainly is that of taxes. Both Australian researchers as mentioned with Scott Bartle and Thomas Anderson have added to the body of evidence exposing this fraud by questioning the validity of this arm of government and of paying taxes in general.

One major issue for anyone having researched the validity of taxation will have come across the question 'If money can be printed out of thin air then why do we need taxes?' The history of income taxation in the west most commonly has reasons of origin in war so as to compensate for the funding of armies etc. some countries such as the U.S. began to have an income tax in 1913 with the establishing of the Federal Reserve, income taxation was at first voluntary in the U.K but parliamentarians eventually made it mandatory.

In Australia's case Income tax began in 1936 of which Scott Bartle asks how did the county survive beforehand? Recollecting the events of the 1930s as examined should largely help answer that question. Another point of issue is that income tax is really meant to be voluntary in a number of countries, certainly concerning the Australian Tax Office (ATO) who's own literature even states -

'The tax system is based on taxpayers complying with the tax laws voluntarily and cooperating with us.'

It has however been the experience of some in Australia as many a place elsewhere in the west, that if one does not comply face coercion and threat of fines and imprisonment. Both Scott Bartle and Thomas Anderson have had their own approach to questioning the validity of the ATO. Scott's approach being to ask proof of validity of the ATO as a legitimate department of the de jure Government of the Commonwealth of Australia and thus Parliament of that Commonwealth as stated in the Act of 1900 of which they asked the following:

- Is the ATO lawfully constituted by the parliament named and defined within the Commonwealth of Australia Constitution Act 1900 (UK)?

- Does the ATO exclusively serve Government of the Commonwealth as referenced within the Commonwealth of Australia Constitution Act 1900 (UK)?

- Is today's Office of the Governor-General a Parallel Office to the Office of Governor-General and Commander-in-Chief of the Commonwealth of Australia established 29 Oct 1900? – If so, how do the Acts the ATO rely upon have any validity?
- Is the Taxpayer a living being to the exclusion of all others?

- Can the Taxpayer perform manual labour and expend effort?

The last two questions will become more relevant to those who don't know what they imply when we examine what has become referred to as the 'STRAWMAN' in legal research circles, essentially being the 'Persona' each of us are issued to interact with the legal reality for such things as taxes.

The approach of Thomas Anderson is a bit more detailed, rather than addressing the matter from the head (the Act that founded government) they instead devised a questionnaire to be issued to ATO authorities in the case of being a sole trader as to prove any valid obligation to pay taxes on the grounds of differentiation between the legal Persona i.e. STRAWMAN and a flesh and blood human being and so which one do the ATO distinguish as the tax payer and on what grounds. Anderson sought the feedback of the ATO as per its Tax Payers Charter however the response of the chosen ATO representative though of a high managerial position it appears were unable to give a full and satisfactory response to the particulars of a sole trader being classified as an individual, where by legal definition a sole trader is a person who is a member of an organisation of a securities exchange. A "sole trader" as an "individual" according to Australian Corporation Law of 1989 must take to mean a person who is a member organisation of a securities exchange, of which Anderson argues a living being cannot be either an organisation, legal entity or a person as a corporation. Anderson also cites the Australian 'Levy on Income Tax' in the context of persons being defined in the same manner where it states –

> "Upon the taxable income derived during the year of income by any person, whether a resident or a non-resident."

Anderson in their approach refer also to legal definitions of words pertaining to the expressing of authority by ATO as the basis of their response to rejecting this presumption, of what is effectively a social contract, where illustrated in their book '*Strawman Illusion*' pg.70 -

> "The ATO provides advice and collects information relating to obligations under the Income Tax Act 1986. It promotes and supports legislation and laws made by the Government and Commonwealth of Australia. The "Taxpayers Charter - In Detail" outlines "the relationship we seek with the community', and "the more you know and <u>understand these factors</u>, the more confident you'll be in dealing with us."

> The Author hereby states that he <u>DOES NOT UNDERSTAND</u>.

> "Under": In or to a position below or beneath something. In or into a condition of subjection, subordination, or unconsciousness. "Standing": A position from which one may assert or enforce legal rights and duties."

Following this Anderson gives the short form for the universal conditions of contract law pg.71 -

> "For a valid contract to be enforced, there are a number of basic rules which must be followed: "A contract is any legally-enforceable promise or set of promises made by one party to another and, as such, reflects the policies represented by freedom of contract In the civil law contracts are considered to be part of the general law of obligations."

Among the questions the ATO failed to answer, and those they could include:

- Can the ATO sue a living being to collect an alleged debt.

- What is the ATO definition of an entity, is a flesh and blood person an entity.

- Unable to explain what a sole trader is.

- Unable to answer if a flesh and blood person is a member organisation of a securities exchange.

- Unable to answer who does an ABN (Australian Business Number) represents upon being obtained as a sole trader, being either the entity, tax agent, flesh and blood person who fills out the form, all of the above or some other.

- Is a Person a flesh and blood human being.

- Stated that a PERSON(S) were a corporation or another organisation in context.

- Have they read and understood the INCOME TAX ACT 1986

- Have they read and understood the CORPORATIONS ACT 2001 (this they answered as irrelevant)

- In consideration of the above questions was it true to say that the ATO can only levy taxes and gain authority over a flesh and blood natural human being by voluntary or assumed agreement and by the transformation of that person into an ENTITY known as a PERSON or TAXPAYER?

From the conclusion of the questionnaire Anderson could only summarize resolutely the ATO is a fraudulent entity operating on misinformation, and by right should be shut down immediately. In reference to the last question on the list, a well know term in contract law is what's called 'meeting of the minds' with both parties being open and transparent as to place both on equal footing in all stipulations, otherwise the contract becomes null and void with the basis for their evidence there being no social contract between they and the ATO in its failure to distinguish the living being from the STRAWMAN Persona in the instance of a sole trader. By this result Anderson conclude there to be no definitive grounds for taxation where saying again in their book 'Strawman Illusion' pg.70 -

> 'The Author, having taken as much care as possible to investigate this matter, cannot therefore be held responsible for any claim of TAX avoidance, or otherwise, as he has taken reasonable steps to establish the facts. The Author claims that in the event that no relationship can be proven to exist between the ATO and the Author, any prior relationship must therefore have been fraudulent, and is void by way of misrepresentation and coercion and all signatures that may have been provided are hereby rescinded.'

The author cannot conform if Thomas Anderson have ever put these findings into practice in refusing to 'contract' with the ATO. Nowhere in their interviews or publications do they state this have however helped create the groundwork for more questioning and expositions from others to follow.

FURTHER EVIDENCE AGAINST THE ATO

In the course of their research Anderson came across earlier correspondences between a number of others and the ATO in questioning the foundations of its validity. The first of which being a court case between an individual and an ATO employee in the case of Ivan Gorshkov v Stephen Chapman Deputy Commission of Taxation, where admitted by Chapman among Gorshkov's allegations that the ATO indeed was not a legal entity.

Further cases include a letter of correspondence from a Mr. Darryl O'Bryan in March of 2001 after receiving a response letter from an ATO Deputy Commissioner of Taxation for their termination of payment of GST and personal income tax on the grounds of proof of the illegality of the ATO being stated from another case of Mceliker v Chapman. The letter from the Deputy Commissioner responds with the following -

> "The fact that the ATO is not a legal entity does not however invalidate any taxation legislation nor any legal notices issued under powers granted to the Commissioner by those taxation Acts."

However, as proof of the inherent biases and corruptions found in case law in favour of the establishment (as will be seen in the case of mortgages) the letter refers to another court case presided by a judge Callinan J and their ruling decision for the outcome of yet another case Dooney v Henry 174 ALR in light of the Mceliker v Chapman case -

> "This last allegation and the misconceived claim for relief in respect of can be immediately disposed of. The Australian Taxation Office is not a legal personality, the applicant does not contend that it is, and whether the Australian Taxation Office is or is not a legal personality, is not a matter of the slightest relevance to any issue or efficacious remedy that might be available to the respondent."

This double standard is further exemplified by the Deputy Commissioner of Taxation stating the following in the same response letter, of which speaks for itself -

> "The fact that the ATO is not a legal entity does not allow you to ignore your legal obligations to the Commissioner of Taxation - Furthermore, the Commissioner is not required to communicate with you personally when issuing you with notices or requiring you to perform activities by acts which he administers."

Another letter of correspondence in 1999 between a Mr Cameron and RJ Tomkins an ATO Solicitor details Mr Cameron seeking validity of the ATO under the Freedom of Information Act 1982 for evidence of the term 'income' as defined in the Income Tax Assessment Act 1936 as well as documented proof of the establishment the ATO.

The definition for income was not found in the 1936 Act with definitions only given to mean "income from personal exertion" and "income from property". Tomkins was further and more profoundly unable to find the relevant documents for either request in the ATO library, records management system or archives, nor any evidence of an executive instrument ever being created in ordering the establishment of the ATO from the office of the Governor-General. The only evidence found by Tomkins to validate the ATO when being told was created as a branch of the Commonwealth Public Service by executive instrument in 1973. Officers of the Commonwealth Public Service are assigned to the ATO and the Commissioner of Taxation is put in charge of those officers under the Public Services Act 1922.

Interestingly, Tomkins also mentions due to being unable to find the information for Mr Cameron under the same Public Services Act were obliged to deny them access to this part of their application on the grounds of being unable to locate the requested document! An appeal process was open to Mr Cameron to pursue the matter though at a price, as well as an appeal to the Ombudsman.

Thomas Anderson in the course of their research were able to obtain a copy of the affidavit given by the Commissioner of Taxation present at the appeal hearing of Mr Cameron to the Administrative Appeals Tribunal. In it they stated that in light of searching for the requested information by Mr Cameron of the validity of the ATO no record existed in the ATO's computerized file marking system referring to the creation of the ATO nor could they identify any relevant files. They further stated that relevant heads of government were consulted regarding the establishing of an executive instrument in setting up the ATO with no evidence being found either of which none knew of such certified documents.

BANKING FRAUD
The Mortgage - a case study

The subject of mortgages, securitization and types of, this author feel strongly to be a central part of the line of logical inquiry among what constitute a true legal roadblock to an NLRBE in urgent need of addressing.

The reader of this work is advised to have a general understanding of the fraudulent nature and practices of banking previous to reading the following information, as instead the focus will mainly be on a particular issue of major contention in dealing with the Banking system, being loans and mortgages, specifically residential mortgages. This section will try to be brief and informative as possible in examining this subject as it can be one that is a large, thankfully having the groundwork of Thomas Anderson among others having made it that much quicker and easier to comprehend in the process, and are gratefully acknowledged in bringing their research endeavours to public light.

The significance of the mortgage simply cannot be understated as being at the heart of the legal and financial everyday mechanisms used to maintain the status quo of land acquisition and use, thus keeping land out of the rightful hands of humanity and into that of the ruling powers, in turn perpetuating wealth/rule divide along with the coveted control and stagnation of the economical, scientific and technological means and resources to assist humanity into a sustainable future of an NLRBE. In short the average residential mortgage is quite literally the backbone, most certainly where the west is concerned, of the entire commercial/monetary system. Without the masses slaving away a majority of their adult livelihoods paying off a mortgage would mean inevitable collapse of one major leg of the banking system and have a domino effect of often catastrophic proportions, as witnessed with the recent GFC of 2007/08 the effects of which are still being felt across the west at this time of writing in 2017.[78]

As stated previously without land there is nothing else, it is the ultimate prerequisite.

Having already examined and established just how land has come to be utilised and owned for centuries and how serious and issue it is, we will now examine one of the key means in which this is maintained in the modern age, that is the mortgage.

DISSECTING THE MORTGAGE

The word Mortgage is a French Law term meaning "dead pledge," apparently meaning that the pledge ends either when the obligation is fulfilled or the property is taken through foreclosure. A mortgage is a security interest in real property held by a lender as a security for a debt, usually a loan of money. While a mortgage in itself is not a debt, it is the lender's security for a debt. A mortgage loan is a loan secured by real property through the use of a mortgage note, which evidences the existence of the loan and the encumbrance of that real property through the granting of a mortgage, which secures the loan.

A mortgage note or instrument, is a promissory note of the mortgage loan. It is a written promise to repay a specified sum of money plus interest at a specified rate and time to fulfill that promise. While the mortgage itself pledges the title to real property as security for a loan, the mortgage note states the amount of debt and the rate of interest obligating the borrower who signed the note as personally responsible for repayment.

---

[78] http://www.independent.ie/business/personal-finance/property-mortgages/mortgage-arrears-problem-still-real-nine-years-after-house-prices-started-to-fall-34526239.html
http://www.theaustralian.com.au/business/economics/mortgage-stress-on-the-rise-standard-poors/news-story/e1a1109cf73d68140511de7af5d87a8b?nk=57432d5a97226faeb2022624f6de2a5d-1497022089

Among the key issues of contention with the mortgage process having come under scrutiny of late, is the whereabouts of the original mortgage note and requesting the Lender to produce the note as evidence that they are the true owners of the debt and therefore deserve payment. Further investigation of the issue some if not all readers may be aware, leads to uncovering the way in which the modern global mortgage and securities industry indeed operates, with the mortgage-backed securities disaster at the heart of the 2007/08 recession and housing market collapse being the perfect example. The following are among the means of operation for the mortgaging process. This example is taken from the U.S model however elements of which are essentially universal.

NEGOTIABLE INSTRUMENTS AND SECURITIZATION

A negotiable instrument is a specialized type of contract for the payment of money unconditional and capable of transfer by negotiation. As payment of money is promised later the instrument itself can be further used by a holder as money in due course.

A holder in due course is a person who takes a negotiable instrument, such as a promissory note, for value, in good faith, without knowledge of any apparent defect in the instrument nor any notice of dishonor. The original creditor then sells the credit contract (the right to receive repayment of the loan) to a new creditor and the new creditor takes the debt for value, in good faith, without any knowledge of a defect in the note, and on it goes.

Further means of action within the mortgage process include Service Release Premiums (SRP), Standing and Securitisation. The Service Release Premium is the payment received by a bank or retail mortgage lender on the sale of a closed mortgage loan to the secondary mortgage market. Standing is the term used for the issue of the legal right to sue being raised and the foundation of what is called the "produce the note" strategy by lenders.

Securitisation for those not too familiar essentially is the creation and issuance of debt securities, or bonds whose payments of principal and interest are derived from cash flow generated by separate tranches (or pools) of assets, which include residential mortgages. Securitisation is commonly used by financial institutions and businesses of all kinds to immediately realize the value of cash-producing assets such as loans, but can also be trade receivables or leases. By pooling assets together, the payment streams can be used to support interest and principal payments on debt securities. The terms for securitized mortgages are known as mortgage-backed securities (MBS) also being the case for Residential Mortgage Backed Securitization (RMBS). Securitized assets, non-mortgage loans or assets with expected payment streams are known as asset-backed securities (ABS). To initiate a securitization a company must first create a special purpose vehicle (SPV). The SPV is actually legally separate from the company or holder of the assets that are then sold to the SPV as part of the profit making process. The payment streams generated by the assets can then be repackaged to back an issuing of bonds or, the SPV can transfer the assets to a trust. In both cases, the bonds are exchanged with an underwriter for cash. The underwriter then sells the securities to investors.

Unlike other bonds, securities backed by mortgages usually pay both interest and a portion of the investor's principal on a monthly basis, most likely explains the popularity of the whole process within the banking world and it being central to a countries general economic health, but as the 2007/08 recession proved became too heavily relied upon being so easy to manipulate for quick gains, essentially being abused as short-term profits for long-term pains

THE REMIC

REMICs (Real Estate Investment Conduits) are investment vehicles used to hold commercial and residential mortgages in trust and issue securities representing an undivided interest in these mortgages. A REMIC assembles mortgages into pools and issue what are called pass-through certificates, multiclass bonds similar to a collateralized mortgage obligation (CMO), or other securities to investors in the secondary mortgage market. Mortgage-backed securities issued through a REMIC can be either debt financings of the issuer or a sale of assets. Notable examples of major issuers of REMICs are the Federal Home Loan Mortgage Corporation (Freddie Mac) and the Federal National Mortgage Association (Fannie Mae) being the two leading secondary market buyers of conventional mortgage loans in the U.S. as well for privately operated mortgage conduits owned by mortgage bankers, mortgage insurance companies, and savings institutions. Both these institutions were instrumental in the 2007/08 US market collapse due in allowing risky derivatives to be created on the backs of both Mortgage types.

THE SECURITIZATION PIGGYBACK

Particularly in the case of ABS and MBS securitization works by having them represent an interest in the underlying pools of loans or other financial assets securitized by issuers, which is often where the assets originate from. The primary function of all securitization transactions is to isolate the financial assets supporting payments on the ABS and MBS. This ensures payments associated with the securities are derived solely from the pool of assets and not from the originator of the assets. By contrast, interest and principal payments on non-securitized debt are often backed by the ability of the issuing company to generate sufficient cash to make the payments. This is done by other assets being used in further securitizations originating through loans or other revenue-producing assets such as leases.

Other assets, such as the balances due on credit card accounts or a corporation's accounts receivable are also securitized as they too initiate a securitization chain through lenders, credit card companies and others, often retaining a connection to their assets following a securitization while acting as a servicer or a collecting agent on regular loan or lease payments eventually forwarding them to the SPV. These asset transfers are also called a 'true sale' as a critical part of the transfer process from the originator. The proceeds of the securities are remitted to the originator as the purchase price for the assets. If the asset transfer is not a true sale investors are vulnerable to claims against the originator of the assets. The cash flows backing the securities or the assets themselves could be ruled a part of the originator's estate and used to satisfy creditors' claims if a true sale did not occur. Legally separating the assets also protects the originator.

ENTRUSTING THE MIDDLEMAN

The SPV can either be a trust, corporation or form of partnership set up specifically to purchase the originator's assets for the flow of payments, while payments advanced by the originators are also forwarded to investors according to the terms of agreement of the security. Also with some securitizations the SPV is only used to collect assets then transferred to another entity (usually a trust) to be repackaged into further securities. The issuing and protection of investors interests in a trust or SVP are then overseen by assigned professionals.

The originator however is still considered the sponsor of the pool. An additional player known as the Underwriter usually an investment bank essentially act as the middleman between the Issuer (SPV or trust) and investors. Their main functions include offering consultation on how to structure the ABS and MBS based on the perception of investor demand as well as advise the SPV in market performance. Underwriters also help determine whether to use their sales network to offer securities publicly or privately. Underwriters also mainly assume the risk associated with buying and reselling of bonds to investors. The field of major securitization vehicles is as broad as it is deep being a vast network of international banks and other hidden parties. To get a further overview and understanding of the securitization process visit the roadblocks to nlrbe website to view and download the diagrams listed on the resource page under the heading mortgage research.

So as not to become potentialy overwhelmed in comprehending this information, it is worth keeping in mind is simply the case of being securities created on the back of securities as a way to help demystify any complexities that might be felt, just as one comprehends the true nature of credit with there being no real money in circulation. Both are just aspects of the same deceptively simple banking fraud perpetrated on the peoples of the world on a daily basis.

As well being a process predicated by numbers on a screen perhaps the other most insulting piece of evidence of this perpetuated is the fact of the originator of assets for investors being the sponsor of the pool, meaning to be among those of low to middle income working and perhaps often struggling to pay residential mortgages in their thousands throughout western countries, and wherever else these practices are taking place, is without question among the lowest and most heinous of crimes being coercively forced on humanity again due to general financial and legal ignorance.

THE TORRENS SERIES

If we recall the Torrens Title, being a system of land ownership developed by Sir Robert Richard Torrens in Australia. Where no document such as a transfer of title or a mortgage is effective until it is recorded at the Land Titles Office. Once your name is registered or recorded on the title register under Torrens title you become the owner of the property to the exclusion of all others, by the very fact of registration, obtaining title by registration. It also prescribes the form and content of documents, which must be used to effect title charges. [79]

A modern day example of application used here again comes from the research of Thomas Anderson. The Torrens Series is the securitization of a portfolio of Australian prime residential mortgages originated by Bendigo and Adelaide Bank (BEN) and National Mortgage Market Corporation, a wholly owned subsidiary of BEN. Below is an excerpt taken from a prospectus titled Second Deed of Amendment, Torrens Series Trust demonstrating an overview of the workings of the Torrens Series.

---

[79] Simply means a term for the price or cost of.

THE SECURITIZATION ROLE PLAYERS

The role and functions of those within the process list as: the Originator, Warehouse lender, Sponsor, Depositor, Trustee, Indenture and Owner Trustee, Primary Servicer, Master Servicer and Master Document Custodian.

The Originator is the lender that provided the funds to the borrower they are essentially the Seller of the loan. It is common practice that some securitize loans and some don't. The decision not to securitize loans may be due to one of three reasons such as lack of access to secondary markets, a business decision not to run the risks associated with future performance with sponsoring a securitization, or the originator obtains better return through another loan disposition strategy such as whole loan sales for cash.

The Originator in turn borrows funds on a line of credit from what is called a warehouse credit facility or "warehouse lender". Warehouse lenders are either what is referred to as "wet" funders or "dry" funders. A wet funder will advance the funds to close the loan upon the receipt of an electronic request from the originator. A dry funder, however will not advance funds until it actually receives the original loan documents duly executed by the borrower. Next is the Sponsor as the lender to securitize the pool of mortgage loans. This makes it the final aggregator of the loan pool before selling the loans directly to **the Depositor**, who in turn sells them to the securitization Trust.

To obtain desired ratings from ratings agencies such as Moody's, Fitch and S&P, the Sponsor is also required to retain some exposure to the future value and performance of the loans depending on what class they may fall into from the highest to lowest rating in the event of sustaining any losses, commonly referred to as the "first loss pieces" of a deal.

The Depositor's main function is to enable types of transaction and state of securitization of mortgage loans. With all structured financial transactions in this process is the mandatory requirement to create at least two "true sales" of the notes and mortgages between the Originator and the Trustee for the Trust to make the assets of the Trust both "bankruptcy" and

"FDIC" remote from the originator. The Depositor purchases the loans from the Sponsor, sells the loans to the Trustee of the securitization Trust, and then uses the proceeds received from the Trust to pay the Sponsor for the Depositor's own purchase of the loans.

Bankruptcy-remote and FDIC-remote are industrial terms for the other institutions who work with the Depositor in this process. A bankruptcy remote company is a company within a corporate group whose bankruptcy has as little economic impact as possible on other entities within the group. A bankruptcy remote company is often a single-purpose entity.

The U.S based Federal Deposit Insurance Corporation (FDIC) uses what is called 'Risk Management of Remote Deposit Capture' to assist financial institutions in identifying risks in their remote deposit capture (RDC) systems and evaluating the adequacy of controls and applicable risk management practices, under which there operate a number of FDIC-Supervised Commercial and Savings banks.

In working with these institutions the Depositor maintains its own separate corporate existence from the Sponsor and the Trust and observe the formalities of this corporate separateness at all times. True sales are further documented by representations and attestations signed by the parties; by attorney opinion letters; by asset purchase and sale agreements as well by proof of adequate and reasonably equivalent consideration for each purchase by true sale reports from the three major ratings agencies of Standard & Poors, Moody's, and Fitch.

The Trustee is the owner of the loan on behalf of the certificate holders at the end of the securitization transaction. As with any trust, the Trustee's powers, rights and duties are defined by the terms of the transactional documents having created the trust, and are subject to the terms of trust laws of the Governing Laws of the territory the trust has been established within. There is also a different non-REMIC structure called an "Owner Trust." In an Owner Trust structure, the Trustee roles are divided between an Owner Trustee and an Indenture Trustee. The Owner Trustee owns the loans while **the Indenture Trustee** has the responsibility of making sure all funds received by the Trust are properly disbursed to the investors (bond holders) and all other parties with a financial interest in the securitized structure.

The Primary Servicer services the loans on behalf of the Trust though a Master Servicing Agreement. A trust can often have more than one servicer servicing portions of the total pool such as through "Secondary Servicers," "Default Servicers," and/or "Sub-Servicers" that service loans in particular categories such as loans that are in default. Any or all of the Primary, Secondary, or Sub-Servicers may be a division or affiliate of the Sponsor. The Servicers are the ones do all the day-to-day work for the Trustee that include sending monthly bills to borrowers, collecting payments, keeping records of payments, liquidating assets for the Trustee, and remitting net payments to the Trustee.

The Master Servicer is the Trustee's representative for assuring that the Servicer abides by the terms of the servicing contract. The Master Servicer has the administrative role in consolidating monthly reports and remittances of funds from individual servicers into a single data package for the Trustee.

If a Servicer fails to perform or goes out of business or suffers a major downgrade in its servicer rating it is part of the Master Servicer's job to find a replacement and assure that no interruptions of essential services are made. Like all servicers, the Master Servicer may be a division or affiliate of the Sponsor but is solely responsible to the Trustee.

The Master Document Custodian takes and maintains physical possession of original hard-copy Mortgage Notes, Mortgages, Deeds of Trust and certain other key loan documents parties deem essential for the enforcement of the mortgage loan in the event of default and for safekeeping to accomplish the transfer and due negotiation of possession essential under Uniform Commercial Code for a valid transfer of the Notes to the Trustee. Like the Master Servicer, the Master Document Custodian is responsible by contract solely to the Trustee yet is an institution wholly independent from the Servicer and the Sponsor.

The Master Document Custodian must review all original documents submitted into its custody for strict compliance with the specifications of a Custodial Agreement and deliver reports to the Trustee and/or Master Servicer as to any required documents that may be missing or fail to comply with specifications. **The Custodian** most importantly must confirm that for each loan in the Trust there is a complete and unbroken chain of transfers and assignments of the Notes and Mortgages. This however does not necessarily require the Custodian to find assignments or endorsements naming the Depositor or the Trustee. In the case of many private-label securitizations a single institution fulfills all of the functions related to document custody for the entire pool of loans. In such cases the institution might be referred to simply as the Custodian and the governing document as what is known as Custodial Agreement.

THE MORTGAGE INSTRUMENT

Recalling our examination of land ownership types, the ongoing implementation of Fee Simple is the basis of typical mortgage situations across the western world being an ongoing and a central issue of injustice and antagonism between the public and banking institutions, typically playing out as follows:

There are two parties to a mortgage, a mortgagor being the owner of the encumbered interest in the real property also known as the borrower and a mortgagee being the lender. Seller's of Mortgages and enforcement of an installment contract can and do vary but as is, installment contracts provide that upon a default by the purchaser, the purchaser loses his or her right to occupy the property, the entire indebtedness is then accelerated through the courts with the purchaser loosing equitable interest in the property and thus forfeited. The seller in this situation does not have to foreclose in order to obtain title to the property. In some cases however what is called a 'quiet title action' is issued if the purchaser has filed the installment contract in local land records and an ejectment action may be necessary to recover possession. Either way it's a win-win for the bank.

ROAMING CHARGES

In the course of their research Anderson found a majority of international Banking Trusts, holding companies, subsidiaries and other Banking entities all being traceable back to either Washington or the State of Delaware in the U.S. meaning the conditions of the trusts fall under the Governing Laws of these territories having their own colours of international commercial law that predominately help perpetuate tax evasion, while the vast majority of residential mortgage backed securitized trusts involved being subject to the applicable trust laws of these territories despite where the physical banks, originators and mortgagors may be in the world. Again if we keep in mind that the legal reality is a system within the framework of Globalization operating in Commerce and thus Admiralty law needing no fixed territory or national allegiance as stated earlier, making for the perfect method of global financial and legal control.

THE CARMEL BUTLER MP MEMORANDUM

In 2009 a report given by U.K MP Carmel Butler to the U.K Treasury Committee which can be found on the U.K Parliament website [80] concerns their investigations of the alleged toxic debts the banking system were said to have incurred during the 2007/08 recession. Butler in their research found this to be untrue and stands proven with comprehensive and in-depth analysis of the legal and systemic fraud within the global mortgage market. They began by saying in their opening statement -

"Let us be clear that the reason for today's injection is the lack of openness and honesty by the banks on the amount of bad debts that they have on their books. The banks have stated their case. They say: the banking crisis ensued from bad borrowers to bad debts to toxic assets to taxpayer support. The banks with their powerful lobby, powerful public relations and easy access to the media have framed the public debate. Consumers on the other hand do not have such powerful infrastructure to effectively rebut the bankers' defamatory accusations. This written evidence challenges the bankers' version and endeavours to dispel the bankers' myths. The chain of events is rooted in lenders' abuse of unfettered power to impose unsustainable interest and charges on consumers combined with their determination to avoid contributing to the public purse."

Where stating secondly -

"The evidence contained in this memorandum is focused on two fundamental issues. Firstly, the consumer issues that arise in the context of Special Purpose Vehicles ("SPVs") that are incorporated as securitisation companies who issued the infamous "toxic-assets"; and secondly, the taxpayer heist at the hand of the SPV securitisations companies. The evidence will illuminate the hitherto hidden truth that the tax payer is supporting the profits of foreign owned companies incorporated in tax havens and their private investors."

---

[80] www.publications.parliament.uk /pa/cm200809/cmselect/cmtreasy/144/144w273.htm

Butler then later give clear evidence of systemic fraud in the use of SVP's -

"There are no bad debts on the banks books. And if there is any bad debt, the amount is de minimis. A primary purpose of a securitisation is: to remove the credit risk from the bank's books. The bank, under a `true sale' will sell all its rights and title in the mortgages to the SPV and the SPV will in return pay the bank cash for the mortgage assets - this plain truth has remained elusive because under the terms of the true sale contract, the bank and the SPVs have unlawfully agreed to keep the transaction concealed from the borrower and, from H.M. Land Registry. Thus giving the false appearance to the world that the banks still own the mortgages."

Further on is explained the legal apparatus in place allowing for such systemic fraud and corruption where given in excellent detail -

"The law provides mortgagees (lenders) with a statutory power to transfer a legal charge. It is under these statutory provisions that the banks exercise their right to assign the mortgages to the SPVs. There can be no doubt that on completion, the buyer has acquired the legal title, but there will inevitably be a "registration gap" between the conveyance date on which the buyer acquired the legal title and the date on which his legal title is registered at H.M. Land Registry.- It is this "registration gap" that the SPV unlawfully exploits in order to conceal its ownership and control of the mortgages.

Emphasising Further -

Under the Land Registration Act 2002 the transferee of a registered charge is required to register at H.M. Land Registry, its ownership of the mortgage that it purchased - therefore, it is a legal requirement that the SPV register its proprietorship of the mortgage at H.M. Land Registry. Whilst the law implicitly permits the registration gap as a matter of pragmatism, the law also implicitly mandates that the registration requirements are to be observed expeditiously. Nonetheless, in contumacious disregard for its legal duty to comply with the registration requirements of the LRA 2002, the contract of sale expressly provides that the SPV will not register the transfer at H.M. Land Registry indeed, the contract provides that notice of the transfer is to be concealed from the borrowers and H.M. Land Registry and a fortiori concealed from the world."

This next paragraph is the crucial point of resolution, effectively summarizing the entire mortgage fraud being perpetrated on the masses, unknowingly slaving their lives away paying off residential mortgages their whole adult lives to banks who don't have any legal right to the mortgage having sold it on to another party and hiding the fact that they are merely administrators -

"The suppression and concealment of this information from H.M. Land Registry is a criminal offence and, in furtherance of this offence, the SPV's legal title to the mortgages is also concealed from the county courts and the Government. The Banks remain registered as the proprietor of the mortgages and accordingly all interested parties are deceived by this concealment with one exception. The SPV does inform its investors that the bank sold its legal title to the SPV (to whom, the right to register the legal title to the mortgages is important). Consequently, the bank appears to be the legal owner, but it is not."

Butler make the example of the former British Building Society Northern Rock in light of the above, in which the British Government ended up selling 13 Billion worth of its Mortgages to a U.S private equity group[81] -

"Northern Rock sold its legal title to the SPV, in this case, to Granite Finance Trustees Limited and therefore, Granite is the legal owner; Northern Rock is the administrator of the mortgages and falsely holds itself out as the legal owner of the mortgages; Granite Finance Trustees Limited should be, but is not, registered as the owner of the mortgage; and all these facts remain concealed because Granite and Northern Rock have unlawfully contracted to suppress this information from H.M. Land Registry."

In conclusion of their findings Butler point to the continued systemic allowances for these continued practices -

---

[81] www.theguardian.com /business/2015/nov/13/northern-rock-mortgages-13bn-sold-us-private-equity

"Notwithstanding that the SPV conceals its legal title from H.M. Land Registry, the SPV will, nonetheless, avail itself of, and exercise, all the statutory and contractual legal powers that the legal owner enjoys. The SPV will exercise the legal owner's statutory power to create a legal charge on the borrower's mortgages. The SPV will register a Legal Charge that the SPV created against the mortgage loans in favour of the SPV's trustee, as security for the payment of money due to its investors and creditors - the SPV's exercise of the legal owner's contractual and statutory legal powers leaves no doubt that SPV is: the legal owner of the mortgages. Nonetheless, the banks and the SPV unlawfully exploit the "registration gap" in a smoke and mirrors tactic to cause confusion and conceal the SPV's legal title. The SPV is the legal owner. The banks are the administrators."

The banks in the U.K as elsewhere in Europe and the U.S received billions in bailouts in the crash of 2007/08 in claiming to be victims of bad borrowers while refusing to disclose these alleged bad debts. In light of the evidences given by Butler it is certainly possible the real reason the banks won't comply is because it would require admitting that they do not own the mortgages which are allegedly bad debts on their books and, they would have to admit that they are falsely registered at H.M. Land Registry as the owner of the mortgages.

The question remains why the U.K Government have yet to make legal changes that require securitization companies to register their ownership of the mortgages at H.M. Land Registry in compliance with section 27 of the Land Registration Act 2002, perhaps it speaks of deeper systemic corruptions, which really altogether is not too surprising given the nature of this whole paradigm.

One final smoking gun in light of Butler's evidence and what with banks keeping cards to their chest, given that as house prices rise mortgages become riskier and thus require more securitization, the more revealed would signal the true health of the market of which the banks would lose face and ensue panic.

Any proof corroborating the fraudulent nature and practices of banking in its present form of debt and speculative laden practices are further confirmation of the self-interest driving this establishment, and ultimately that of institutional preservation. Any evidences the researcher can acquire in presenting to the public the proof of which prove invaluable, but even more so when of this calibre. Coming from official sources within the establishment such as the endeavours of Carmel Butler MP presents hope, clarity and confirmation of exposing such lies and deceit, and strengthen the argument of provably demonstrating the fraud of the banking system and the instruments of debt they use, such as that of the mortgage, specifically the residential mortgage, as among central aspects of a very real and legal road block to a NLRBE.

MICHAEL AND THE MORTGAGE MIRACLE

The following recounts the story of a U.K based legal researcher by the name Michael of Bernicia. In helping to end this topic on a happier note, theirs is a story of how they prevented the bank from repossessing a family property and stands as not only one of the very few examples having won a mortgage case, blatantly exposing systemic fraud within the U.K legal and banking systems along the way. Michael has in fact made their story central to a recent documentary they produced called The Great British Mortgage Swindle and continue to give talks advice the length and breadth of the U.K and for various online alternative media radio shows. Their story begins by examining the fraud of the mortgage process from the very beginning of which relates directly to the land registry issue highlighted in the above evidence of U.K MP Carmel Butler.

Michael quickly noticed that when a Mortgagor authorises what is called a legal charge against a property someone may wish to acquire, is done so under fraud because no equitable or legal rights has yet been granted of any interest over the property i.e. proprietary interest, being a registered proprietor. This immediately already makes the mortgage contract illegal and void. Furthermore, in their research did Michael begin to uncover this mass fraud perpetrating as far back as the 1980s, at least, as even though there was a law in place through the 'Property and Miscellaneous Provisions Act of 1989' prescribing every contract to be signed and executed in the presence of witnesses in one sitting, the majority of mortgage contracts they examined not even having any signatures.

IGNORING OF THE FACTS

They even brought this evidence to light in their own court case of which the Judge outright dismissed as baseless while continually ignoring documented evidence and previous cases showing violation of the 1989 Act. As well as this in the circumstances of their case centring around the bank demanding compound interest payments, Michael responded by asking the bank to produce material evidence of a valid and enforceable contract in existence as well could they prove they in fact had any money to loan, only to be met with silence on such questions only responding with continued statutory demand for the payments, with no evidence to show it was legally enforceable. Michael then through power of Attorney made a claim for fraud against the bank for illegally registered as the receivers of the property. What happened next only adds to the body of evidence of the biased nature of the established institutions enacted through double standard policy and practises, for when Michael tried to make a pay agreement with the bank through a Promissory note-to-Barer being theoretically an entirely valid form of credit as a Promise-to-Pay, of which the bank rejected responding with saying it will decide what form of currency be used for repayment, of which Michael could only conclude to mean 'Sweat Equity'.

Michael pressed on with the case and despite presenting a number of evidential case laws binding to the court and a copy of the document in question trying to be passed off as a contract having no signatures, essentially just being an offer from the bank in the eyes of the law, the judge still continued to reject the evidence saying that the bank didn't need to have signed documentation to enforce a contract while siding with the bank in rejecting the Promissory note to Barer. On top of this the Judge in an attempt to intimidate Michael and shut down the case completely awarded 90,000 pounds in damages to the bank while his family neared bankruptcy. It was at this point however that Michael didn't know about the 1989 Act only discovering it in later research of high court and court of appeal cases.

One of the key things they noticed from the Act was that partial performance by parties for a mortgage was abolished, being the presumption of banks not needing a signed contract only the intention as the mortgagor to enter into a mortgage transaction, of which they had been getting away with, as well using computer printed statements. Michael then took their case to the court of appeal only to be met with more opposition in the form of the Court Funds Office which had the power to accept whatever instruments was tendered when a debt was in dispute and payment had been made in good faith as a valid negotiable security and hold until the bank accepted it. The office rejected the promissory note unless a court order had them do otherwise, being highly unlikely. After this Michael applied for appeal at the Supreme Court to present their case only to be rejected twice.

THE WINNING MOVE

Just when the situation seemed at an end Michael still refused to give in. Next came the piece of information that would win them the case by issuing new proceedings against the bank and receivers on the grounds that a fraud had taken place upon the court, as the bank swore that the mortgage and all others in its book were valid. Michael cleverly new this could not be ignored as it was now a harm being perpetrated upon the establishment itself. The court now all of a sudden was the victim thus making it a claimant against the bank. As well as the evidence of a previous judge having lied in the bank's favour saying the mortgages on its book were all signed.

EVIDENCE FOR INJUNCTION

Though the situation had changed in their favour the case wasn't won just yet. They next went to the land registry to obtain an official registration entry of their family's property where they noticed a huge mistake made by the bank having made a mortgage in the name of the family trust as a limited company when in fact it wasn't, making it the wrong name on the mortgage. Back in court the Judge had to admit this fault and that Michael was in the right with the presentment of such evidence, while making the Judge look even more foolish by having them admit and apologise for not allowing Michael to highlight this evidence at an earlier stage in the case in denying the disclosure of all documents. The Judge then adjourned the case to a specialist judge while Michael issued further criminal proceedings against the bank for fraud on the grounds of false representation, non- disclosure and abuse of position against the receivers to try and prevent a fire sale of the property in the meantime. When their next day in court came Michael once again found their evidence being dismissed with the Judge evidently being on the side of the bank by practically dictating their defence application. The Judge then adjourned the case having appointing themselves to take it up again while issuing a civil restraint order on Michael so that they couldn't perform any more actions against the bank. Certain that the Judge would only dismiss the case on the basis of being without merit they made an informal application to have the Judge Recused (removed from the case) on the grounds of showing prejudice towards they and extreme bias toward the bank, technically making them an advocate. The replacement Judge who took up the case Michael quickly began to suspect were even worse than their predecessor, who in fact would do something to Michael's knowledge and those within the legal community to whom they disclosed their case, unprecedented and wholly illegal.

SAVING FACE AND SAVING GRACE

Michael was convinced by the conduct of the Judge that they had already a preconceived judgement ready and were just 'filling in the blanks' before doing so. Being that they were representing the family trust as beneficiary, as per the Trustee Act of 2000 no beneficiary could act as a representative or agent of a trustee. The Judge went out of their way to brake this rule by making Michael a party to the claim, hence a trustee. This was both unheard of in theory or practice in law or equity. The Judge performed this illegal action for two reasons, so as to impose further civil restraint on Michael and most heinously of all to intentionally bankrupt he and his family and rob them of their property to the hands of the bank.

Despite such despicable deeds within the court system the victory ultimately went to Michael on administrative grounds, as the bank didn't issue a defence against Michael's allegations of fraud against the court within the allotted time frame, most certainly because of not having a leg to stand on, meaning Michael won by default judgement. Michael finally amended the issue of rights to the property through the land registry and had the mortgage struck off. Even though at the time this Judge dismissed the case without merit did they later admit Michael was right and that the provisions of the 1989 Act were correct. This one case alone is self-evident of the depths of myopic arrogance and elitism pervading the establishment. This Judge was consciously willing to bankrupt and make homeless a family rather than admit to being wrong.

To an outsider, clearly this is sociopathic while to an insider a decision of such power as self-evident of the depths its agents are willing to go to in order quash any challenges to their perceived authority so as to prevent any further such uprising or exposure of the corruption.

With the banking system violating the requirement to register their ownership of mortgages at H.M. Land Registry in compliance with section 27 of the Land Registration Act 2002. [82] is proof of such lengths; the system and its agents operate on a fundamental double standard of which many, many further cases could be found if only this study had time to permit in demonstrating and encourage the reader to investigate further for themselves as further proof.

The legal framework without a doubt is THE roadblock to a truly free world, with such agents as Judges we can only expect to meet us as at the tole gates along the way until their power and status are removed and this system along with it.

---

[82] Another point of study for further investigation that for the time being can only be labelled as deliberate and systemic bias and corruption in favour of the banks and compliant parties within government as one of the major frauds perpetuated on the U.K public.

SECTION THREE
THE REALITY

The subject of free will is spoken of time and again mainly on moral, religious and spiritual grounds. However, in light of all we have studied in this work, legal and commercial grounds clearly have the last word. Nothing possible on any material level throughout all facets of earthly life are obtained or achieved without an underlying monetary and/or legal element.

In *The Zeitgeist Movement Defined* are spoken of 'Proxy Systems' as the fundamental basis to the market concept associated to assumptions of human behaviour inlight of traditional values accompanied by an intuitive view of history ignoring the facilitation of any emergent reasoning, public health measures, technical and scientific capacities or true and comprehensive ecological responsibility. Instead we have established notions of the 'free market' and all the factors it houses to resolutely produce responsible, sustainable and humane outcomes led by 'freedom of choice', or to put it more aptly the 'Illusion of choice' as the late comedian and social commentator George Carlin once said.

RULE BY PROXY

The legal reality is at the heart of such Proxy systems, again as described in *The Zeitgeist Movement Defined* to be:

> 'A technical order seen in the world mostly the result of financial processes (and thus legal)* ·that have little to no perception of larger scale outcomes with the driving proxy above all in the world being of course profit, therefore actions are only taken if they are profitable.'

Of the above quote most certainly legal mechanisms can be found at play, for as evidence found in the changes made in western government, banking and commerce of the 1930s were purely for the sake of profit with the majority of acts and statutes being brought into existence continually ever since on predication of profit throughout all levels of society from taxes to banking fees, parking fines and speeding tickets to health and safety permits for land, real estate as well as a plethora of domestic and occupational requirements, namely insurance. This is not to say such precautions of health and safety aren't necessary, but what seems most of all lacking and what government, banking and legal institutions appear devoid of is common sense, that and the argument as upheld by the TZM and others of the avoidances that can be made of such things within existing systems we are continually subjected to by the true and full implementation of a NLRBE.

FACING THE REALITY

A strong reason for the purpose of this work is to help the NLRBE advocator community and those otherwise gain the benefits of insight into the legal reality, who although being fully aware of the futilities and detriments of existent systems and agents within, who foolishly and myopically persist in

---

*   legal emphasis added

preserving such systems, may themselves believe the inevitable progresses of science and technology as enough to eventually 'phase out' the free market, government, banking and all those associated.

This work and its author in light of which extend the invitation of all the more reason to study and become versed in the legal reality while offering a strong word of caution: As long as legal frameworks exist so too will these institutions in one form or another.

Despite whatever amount of technical or scientific progresses are made the legal framework persists to ensure they are, to use a term, 'Ring Fenced' of which numerous cases are to be found, and even to some extent see an amalgamation of the two, although in this example[83] being of advantage to the public as a temporary band aid still will not remove the source of the problem entirely.

---

[83] http://www.telegraph.co.uk/technology/2016/06/29/19-year-olds-robot-lawyer-overturns-160000-parking-tickets

IN VIOLATION OF NATURE

As comprehended by NLRBE advocates, as well as others, there are of course the laws of nature: the natural order. So too, as examined previously in the case of social interaction and relationships there exists a natural order to achieve and maintain balance and harmony as much as possible. Over time this natural order of human relations and cooperation became corrupt and polluted by self-serving parties through manipulative mechanisms and concepts predicated on a monetary element (not surprisingly) such as through creation of fee simple, the mortgage and other securities as well as of course debt through usury/ interest.

We examined also the true definitions and implications of constitution and citizenship while understanding the fundamental differences of freedom and liberty. People have come to fear government due to enforced regulations by acts and statutes to make society comply with demands and regulations. There is no natural justice in dealing with Government, certainly as of the changing events of the 1930s, of which the masses are unwittingly exploited further in not knowing how to defend oneself and constantly told to get legal expertise, again predicated on more financial extortion. Lawyers only respond to current situations of the banks, corporations and Government Vs the people. The BAR Society violate the true study and practices of (Natural) law to have lawyers become specialists in social regulation, while making the word "law" synonymous with politically imposed or sanctioned social regulation.

The current legal system as mentioned briefly before, also takes away personal liability by creating legal personas to hide behind often leading to rampant abuses such as bank bailouts and avoidance of environmental and social crimes by corporations and other commercial entities. An everyday example of which being the public manipulated into buying insurance for a whole range of issues as just another example of the nature of the legal reality to remove more and more personal liability, self-awareness and self-determination by taking away freedom of choice and movement in fear of 'maybe' causing harm to another due to the very inefficiencies of the system to begin with, as indeed a further double con and another means of extortion of one's wealth, time and energy in life.

TRUST IN WE

This leads us onto the topic of Trusts, proof being in the name. It is so obvious as described in the previous chapter, how society has gradually become manipulated and conditioned away from natural patterns of relationship and interaction to become a purely monetized operation so as not to trust one another. Everything predicated on the monetary element within the legal reality of credit and securities and all other dealings thereafter, are one big confidence trick we've all been lead to falsely believe and abide in, creating more unnecessary fear and hostility with continued stresses and anxieties. This being an intricate part of Commerce also, based essentially on problems and the solving of those problems through mistakes and inefficiencies of others, in endless chains of time and resource wasting events and scenarios.

An excellent insight again given in *The Zeitgeist Movement Defined* explains this to be 'built-in pressures' to avoid socially easing interests so as to avoid loss of profit i.e. the more there is to service and capitalize upon and sustain economic 'growth.' The featuring of the legal concept and use of Trusts as banded about in the course of this work, although readers may have made the educated guess of what it means, is worth reiterating in more detail. The concept of a Trust stems from a very natural consequence of human interactions and relationships that occur for all manner of reason and circumstance. If a friend or relative wished to borrow something from you they agree to return it within a certain time, you have just formed a Trust. Like all other elements of Natural Law the legal reality has confiscated and manipulated the trust relationship such as with the mortgage and securities.

The parties of a Trust are as follows:

The creator also referred to as the Grantor. Then there is the Settlor as the one who brings the needed asset into the trust to pass to its beneficiaries. They may or may not be the Creator. The Trustee has legal title to settle all liabilities as a paid agent for their services. The Beneficiary is the one with possessory title/right to trust corpus. It is possible for the Beneficiary to be the creator of the trust. There is a key difference in having possessory and legal title. To have possessory (equitable) title means to hold something without necessarily having (legal) ownership.

Given how the Trust is central to this commercial and legally driven world speaks of its very nature, being of the fact that anything we do in this world is subject to uncertainty. Again those within the NLRBE advocator community and others likewise may know the reason for this to be due to inbuilt inefficiencies and inadequacies of its very framework and the solutions a NLRBE can offer counter to this.

One does not have to cry conspiracy to witness the evidence as featured in this work of how such Trust relationships have been manipulated to serve the powers-that-be through ignorance and fear of the masses while being denied their natural rights as human beings. The following diagrams demonstrate the relationship between society and government as under corporate de facto 'government' and how it rightly should be under de jure constitutional government as servants of the public. The same could be said for the greater socioeconomic sphere in regards to the legal reality likewise.

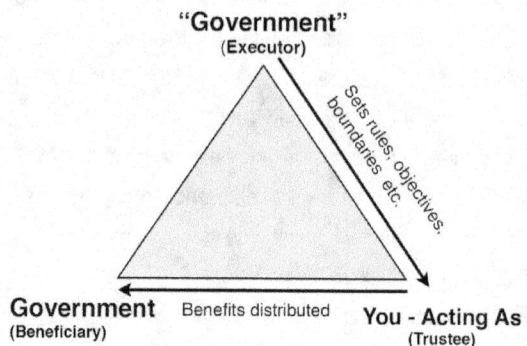

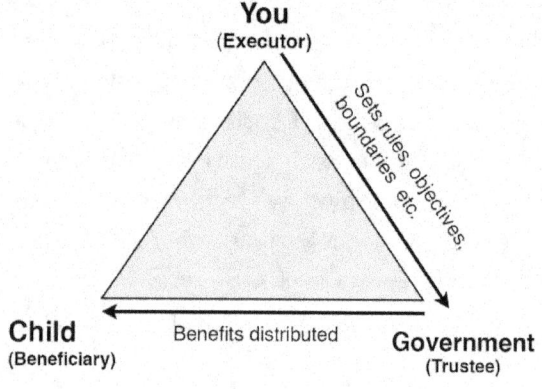

The Trust triangle

DERIVING FROM NATURE

An additional worthwhile piece of insight while on the subject of natural systems of law being usurped by the legal reality is that of derivatives. To again quote the work and research of U.S based legal and financial veteran researcher Winston Shrout they offer a perspective of how the perverted logic of the system manipulates our everyday lives on a number of key socioeconomic levels through such means.

In taking the example of a derivative as being anything but zero, in the laws of nature everything likewise tries to bring itself into balance i.e. homeostasis; achieving zero, and so any socioeconomic system that uses the inspiration of nature/natural systems has the chance of success and thrive. Anything other than this leaves a derivative to deal with. This is a major flaw in the man-made creation of accountancy and commercial dealings in the use of double entry book keeping in striving to achieve and maintain similar zero balance and can only be seen as futile in addition to a debt and securities based financial system, adding to the proof that our world cannot be maintained indefinitely on such a volatile system and further call for a NLRBE. future issues.

Before moving ahead to our final subjects of examination other further issues unable to be included at length include copyright, patents and intellectual property as yet more legal road blocks to a NLRBE as means to 'ring fence' scientific and technological advances for greater socioeconomic application in the welfare and prosperity of humanity.

There is also the case of legal manipulations by tech and other online companies such as Google, Apple, Microsoft and Facebook among the main players having effectively turned the public into commodities for clients to target with marketing and advertising, while cooperating with government intelligent agencies where concerning user privacy and data control as proof of yet another micro endemic of manipulated public gullibility and ignorance within the macro legal reality. The documentary

'Terms and Conditions Apply' by Collin Hoback is a good starting point for further research.

FREEMAN VS STRAWMAN

We will now look at those who have tried to question and scrutinize the establishment in its uses and abuses of the legal reality while trying to find escape and exclusion from its jurisdiction through non-violent and passive solutions and remedies.

Those involved have come to be known or associated under various headings such as Freeman, lawful rebellion, and commercial remedy/redemption. Notable individuals who have shared their research and experience having arose from what could rightly be described as a movement include Robert Menard and Dean Clifford of Canada, Winston Shrout, Mark Stevens and Karl Lentz from the U.S, Michael of Bernicia and the late John Harris of the U.K as well as Thomas Anderson, Scott Bartle and Frank O'Collins from Australia.

Although it must be noted not all fall under the above headings nor should they be labelled as such, but what they all have in common is the questioning of authority and legitimacy of government, the banks and other commercial institutions so as to not simply accept these alleged authorities' prima facie. Though it has been well documented some have not always been correct or successful in their approach or findings, having indeed made mistakes, some serious in fact impacting the lives of them, their families and others unfortunately. In time to come however they may well be regarded as trailblazers, as there are no guidebooks or set methods to follow often just hard research of the legal framework with trial and error. There are also other numerous individuals, online video uploads, transcripts, radio shows, blogs and chat rooms dedicated to the discussion and advancement of this area, some in favour while others debunking it.

We should also keep in mind that over-all it is the healthy questioning and scrutinizing of authority and how it operates to be the take away, although their actions may at times be mistaken or misguided in practice have at least helped expose the façade of alleged authority while reminding us to be ever aware, sceptical and critical and to rightly demand truth and resolution in the name of humanity.

THE FREEMAN MOVEMENT

The term Freeman originates from the description of those who in medieval days were not tied to land under medieval serfdom (government service), unlike a villein or serf. In the year 1297 this term was used in the Magna Carta. Perhaps the most famous clause of Magna Carta states:

> 'No "Freeman" shall be taken or imprisoned, or be disseised of his Freehold, or Liberties, or free Customs, or be outlawed, or exiled, or any other wise destroyed; nor will We not pass upon him, nor condemn him, but by lawful judgment of his Peers, or by the Law of the Land.'

This is sometimes called the "law of the land clause", thus the reasoning for the "on the land" from the statement "freeman on the land"; to establish the fact that I am a free man, of flesh and blood, standing on dry land ruled by the law of the land, or common law. The complete opposite of " law of the water", or Admiralty law if we recall was originally designed for commercial use on the high seas to govern corporations having since been adapted for use on dry land law under the guise of colorable law used in globalization.

Given as one of the prime arguments by subscribers to the Freeman concept stemming from the Magna Carta a modern day court case of 'Essenberg v The Queen B54/1999 [2000] HCATrans 385 (22 June 2000)' however had the Judge rejects to such claims with the following -

> "I understand that and persons who have not had full legal training often think of Magna Carta and the Bill of Rights as fundamental documents which control governments, but they do

not. After all, Magna Carta was the result of an agreement between the barons and King John and the barons themselves had their own courts, had their own armies, they, in effect, levied what we would call taxes today and they were concerned to protect themselves against the growth of the central power of the royal government, the central government, and that is how Magna Carta came into existence, but modern Parliament did not arise until late in the 17th century and the early struggle was between the King and the barons. We are dealing now with the question of the legislature. I mean, Parliament established its authority over the monarch after the struggles which led to the execution of Charles I and the flight from the kingdom of James II in 1688."

The fundamental modern concept otherwise for the Freeman movement, being that the legal (Statutory) system doesn't apply to them and therefore none of its rules and regulations without consent, instead only complying with Common - (natural) - law. Furthermore, are questions regarding the power of the legal system over oneself such as:

- Why should I be subject to the laws of the country

- I was born in if I never chose to be born there?

- I don't agree with a law, and I don't think I should have to comply – what power do you have to make me follow it?

- Why should I have to comply with laws that were implemented by a government I didn't vote for?

- Why should anyone be able to force me how to behave? Why does (or should) anyone have that power over me?

A main point of contention by mainstream critiques and debunkers of the movement in light of the above is the consenting to legislative acts and statutes, yet despite being aware among both legal philosophers and practitioners that acts and statutes are given the force of law by consent of the governed. Those who debunk this view perhaps do so on the assumption of how modern day government is structured and operates, with citizens not being actively engaged in every piece of act and statute brought into legislation obviously being the job of elected politicians. Again there is also the movement's rejection of the type of legal framework in place that mainstream critics debunk the movement for, being the Statutory-admiralty based system and the relevance of events from the 1930s as examined in this work and the significance of the court case of Erie Railroad v. Tompkins in 1938.

There is also the reality of what being a citizen and therefore subject to constitution really means as stated by a Professor of legal philosophy with von Brun in their essay as quoted earlier, which again a number of these mainstream critiques seem totally unawares as a fundamental point of origin for the movement's claim of protest and non- cooperation.

The questioning of being subjected to the jurisdiction of a country and therefore government one did not choose to partake in electing are rightly valid and obvious questions deserving of a response but criticized by debunkers and naysayers as irrelevant, apparently too simple to be deserving of merit. Such questions do of course place the validation of government into question as a whole, if one where never even to learn that government has become a full- fledged commercial operation as a corporate de facto entity, the purpose and performance of government in the west has more and more become questionable over time by not holding up its end of 'social contract' between it and the citizenry, with diminishing quality of life and questionable standards of living, while more often than not serving corporate and banking interests first.

THEIR COURT THEIR RULES

If we recall the mortgage case of Michael of Bernicia the resolution required a self- harm to the establishment before it admit to being wrong, similarly does one think information that questions the very existence of government would be made available to agents and potential agents throughout mainstream education and workplace similarly would those at the lower levels of banking be made aware of what fractional reserve lending is, as well the fraudulent nature of the institution that provides them a living.

The Freeman and others of similar standing simply have the advantage of outsider perspective. The BAR Society as stated earlier violate the true study and practices of (Natural) law to have lawyers become specialists in social regulation, while making the word "law" synonymous with politically imposed or sanctioned social regulation of which students and practitioners are indoctrinated into accepting and protecting as agents of the establishment.

DEBUNKERS AND STATE APOLOGISTS

A few of the examples used by impassioned state apologist debunkers [84] who one can only guess suffer a form of Stockholm syndrome use court cases as an absolute prima facie to any Freeman floundering, the first of which they point out to be the STRAWMAN 'myth' citing Section 3 of a 1996 case United States v. Washington -

> "Finally, the defendant contends that the Indictment must be dismissed because 'KURT WASHINGTON,' spelled out in capital letters, is a fictitious name used by the Government to tax him improperly as a business, and that the correct spelling and

---

[84] thelastbastille.wordpress.com /2014/02/03/only-on-paper-the-pathetic-story-of-commercial- redemption-freemen-on-the-land-sovereign-citizens-lawful-rebellion-community-immunity/

presentation of his name is 'Kurt Washington.' This contention is baseless."

Other evidence saying also that the capitalizing all the letters of your legal name is simply an attempt to "ensure uniformity and good appearance" on government documents - [85]

> "The general principle involved in the typography of datelines, addresses, and signatures is that they should be set to stand out clearly from the body of the letter or paper that they accompany. This is accomplished by using caps and small caps and italics, as set forth below. Other typographic details are designed to ensure uniformity and good appearance. Street addresses and ZIP Code numbers are not to be used. In certain lists that carry ZIP Code numbers, regular spacing will be used preceding the ZIP Code. Certain general instructions apply alike to datelines, addresses, and signatures."

Contrary evidence shows a definition from the legal dictionary Blacks law to be the following -

> A "front"; a third party who is put up in name only to take part in a transaction. Nominal party to a transaction; one who acts as an agent for another for the purpose of taking title to real property and executing whatever documents and instruments the principal may direct respecting the property. Person who purchases property, or to accomplish some purpose otherwise not allowed. [Black's Law Dictionary, Sixth Edition, p 1421]

The fact that countries which originally hold Common law to be their foundational system have over time become bastardized in statutory law as reiterated numerous times throughout this work with the changing events of the 1930s and the example of the 1938 Erie Railroad v. Tompkins case. As well as this the system perpetuates the practice of Case law as part of Common law. A major aspect of this is that judgments given by higher (appellate) courts in interpreting statutes (namely provisions of a

---

[85] www.gpo.gov/fdsys/pkg/GPO-STYLEMANUAL-2008/pdf/GPO-STYLEMANUAL-2008.pdf

constitution) applicable in cases brought before them. These precedents binding on all courts within the same jurisdiction are followed as the law in similar cases. Over time, these precedents are recognized, affirmed, and enforced by the subsequent court decisions, thus continually expanding the common law.

The Judge however will often have the final say and decide what stands as law, and as we have seen with the example of the mortgage case of Michael of Bernicia for all intents and purposes the Judge and court appeared as corrupt in effort to save the establishment from sustaining a loss or harm. A general comprehension among these movements is to try seek remedy wherever natural rights prevail within the court hierarchy.

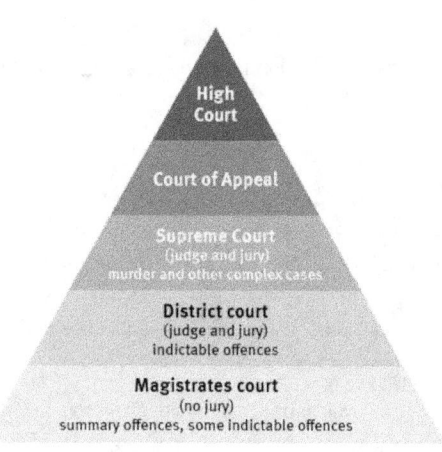

The Court hierarchy system

LAWFUL REBELLION

Lawful rebellion is in many ways related to the Freeman movement in that it works on the premise of finding remedy and alternatives to the modern statutory system through Common (natural) law to both protect and preserve one's self and property. Being mostly prevalent and indeed having originated in the U.K through historical connections to the Magna Carta of 1215 and Declaration of Rights of 1688. The Lawful Rebellion website introductory information describes the justification of which to be based upon article 61 of the Magna Carta Constitutional Security Clause, to protect the people from a corrupt or despotic government providing lawful authority to refuse to cooperate with any Crown agency. It then explains that Article 61 was invoked by petitioning of all members of the House of Lords by the Magna Carta Society in 1999.

A Committee of the Barons was formed and served notice on The Sovereign in March 2001. The research paper that led to the Petition can be viewed here.[86] The Queen failed to respond within 40 days according to her constitutional and contractual duty (Coronation Oath) with a representative claiming that she was bound to follow the instructions of Her ministers and had no veto.[87] The movement none the less state that the terms of Article 61 (lawful rebellion) will remain in force until a Constitutional Convention decides otherwise. Details of what Lawful Rebellion constitutes are given as follows:

> "Anyone who has taken their Oath of Allegiance possesses immunity from any crown or parliamentary mandate, law etc. if committed with the express intention of distressing/detraining the Crown under A.61 This is called "Lawful Excuse." (But they are NOT excused from common-law crimes and torts, except under duress of circumstance)."

---

[86] http://magnacartasocietyblog.blogspot.co.uk/2011/06/magna-carta-society-research-paper.html
[87] Recalling the changes having been made to the Queen to be now both a 'Statutory Monarch' and purely titular.

These include:

- ALL Britons without exception are obliged by the common law to stand in lawful rebellion or be compelled to do so.

- All Britons have a constitutional / common law

- OBLIGATION to disrupt Crown operations/activities to the best of their abilities.

- All Britons have a constitutional / common law OBLIGATION to withhold taxes to the best of their abilities.

- All Britons have a constitutional / common law OBLIGATION to seize government buildings and assets and retain possession until redress of grievance to the best of their abilities. This could be any Crown building including Courts, police stations, town halls.

The movement claim to have continued success with those to take the oath to uphold lawful Rebellion with court summonses, warrants of arrest and criminal custodial sentences all be rebutted with impunity. Debunking of the lawful Rebellion has been based mainly upon the argument of interpretation of Article 61 of the Magna Carta with a member of TPUC.org [88] as founded by the previously mentioned late John Harris even stating –

> "John's idea of Lawful Rebellion is very much based on Magna Carta, article 61. We know now that it was never intended that it be used by the people, and no-one, it would appear, has gained much here or there through claiming or refuting status, or much other paper-based action."

Saying further -

> "When your intent is good you may think that you are given super powers, and to a degree, this is true. But the intent of a rigged system, with rigged politics, rigged courts, and pirates on the

---

[88] http://www.lawfulrebellion.org/2012/10/28/john-harris-suit-jacket-or-straight-jacket/

rigging of UNITED KINGDOM PLC corporate vessel is to obey the captain, and the captain has command."

TUG OF WAR

As with the Freeman movement those active in Lawful Rebellion it seems for the foreseeable future will continue to be engaged in an everyday legal and lawful tug of war with institutional powers of the state, claiming a victory here a victory there as however a slow and sporadic process without any real monumental change or shake up to the establishment, serving as band aids effectively.

Though some would argue change can only be effected within each of our lives and local communities; that we shouldn't expect anything revolutionary or indeed evolutionary any time soon, which is true to a point and proves ultimately that engaging and trying to find remedy from the establishment is a futile process as after all to be 'their' system of which they can change the goal posts as they wish.

This is again proven further with methods of remedy popular within the freeman movement being debunked rooted in the UCC of NOUICOR (Notice of Understanding and Intent and a Claim of Right) and A4V (Accepted for Value). The intention of the NOUICOR is to deny consent to be governed through what is termed 'lawful excuse' while including in the instance of dealing with a government agent a fee schedule typically a cop who has harassed or arrested them excessively in an attempt to make them truly accountable for their actions by making them pay with money.

Debunkers point to this method being repelled in Canada as of 2012 under Section 39 of the Criminal Code of Canada while no known justification to exist in the U.S. while further debunking arguments say the term 'Notice of Understanding' has no legal meaning unless the context demands that it evidences a meeting of the minds for the purposes of contract formation, being a well-settled principle of common law that in order to be bound by a contract, there must be an agreement. Put simply, one cannot bind someone simply by sending them a Notice unless it is a right conferred by some earlier statute or legislation, or legally binding agreement. The issue of the AV4 plays into another area we will come to examine next related to another aspect of the movement called 'Commercial Redemption' that the Birth Certificate is purportedly a financial security and by using the A4V method can one access it to discharge debts. A quote issued from the U.S. Treasury's Officer of Inspector General used by debunkers however states otherwise -

> "The Department of the Treasury is also aware of several fraudulent schemes that involve what are claimed to be securities issued or backed by the Treasury Department or another part of the U. S. Government...another scheme is a variation of a common fraud generally known as 'redemption' or 'acceptance for value' that incorrectly asserts the United States government has trust accounts linked to each citizen. The theory is not supported in fact or law and has been soundly rejected by the federal courts. Perpetrators will annotate or stamp invoices with 'Accept for Value' or similar language, with various numbers purporting to be account numbers. Such annotations are without merit and establish no rights or privileges in any federal or state account or agency."

While the following statement from the FBI [89] is given of the matter -

> "Proponents of this scheme claim that the U.S. government or the Treasury Department control bank accounts – often referred to as 'U.S. Treasury Direct Accounts' – for all U.S. citizens that can be accessed by submitting paperwork with state and federal authorities. Individuals promoting this scam frequently cite various discredited legal theories and may refer to the scheme as 'Redemption,' 'Strawman,' or 'Acceptance for Value.' Trainers and websites will often charge legal fees for 'kits' that teach individuals how to perpetrate this scheme. They will often imply that others have had great success in discharging debt and purchasing merchandise such as cars and homes. Failure to implement the scheme successfully are attributed to individuals not following instructions in a specific order or not filing paperwork at correct times."

---

[89] https://www.fbi.gov/scams-and-safety/common-fraud-schemes

HACKING THE GAME

As previously mentioned there are no established textbooks, tutorials or how-to-do's in place in dealing with this subject, only trial and error being the mark of achievement and progress as many of the figures having been discussed and mentioned within this work would attest to. Due to the fact that we in society, just as with the truths of finance, have never been taught how to engage the system in comprehending and navigating its traps and pitfalls. As with any of these movements new comers risk becoming too over ambitious and brave in their desire to practice and preach without the adequate time and knowledge to fully master and comprehend the subject matter, while sceptics and naysayers watch on the sidelines ever critical. No one, unless through ambition and eagerness would want to have to sit down and study copious volumes of act and statute, to study governmental structure and administration of how the legal system and courts work without a very good reason; in short its boring and tedious, and why there are paid professionals instead who do it. Yet as is often the case, once the seemingly complicated veil is lifted the truth can be simple, and so solutions likewise can be simple. A number of individuals who have adopted a K.I.S.S (Keep It Simple Stupid) methodology are Mark Stevens, Nathan Fraser and Karl Lentz from the U.S.

Mark Stevens is a legal researcher, educator and essayist with many years of experience in and out of court having written two books chronicling this journey with *Adventures in Legal land* and *Government Indicted*. They also host a regular radio show called The No State Project. Mark's approach is inspired by the Lysander Spooner[90] philosophy of non-consent based upon having never explicitly had a hand or say in forming the U.S federal constitution and so not recognizing or conforming to its laws. Mark's approach is a two-step process:

---

[90] Lysander Spooner was a Nineteenth Century American individualist anarchist, political philosopher, essayist, pamphlet writer, Unitarian Christian abolitionist, supporter of the labour movement, legal theorist, and entrepreneur.

1) What proof is there that a jurisdiction applies to me?

2) Show me the facts of that proof as evidence.

Mark applies this strategy from the top down of government, having dealt mainly with taxes as well as speeding and parking fines and such have come to the conclusion that the institute of government has come to resemble no more than a legal criminal syndicate in its display of extortion and coercion to the body politic. Time and again when applying this method have they received mere assertions and beliefs of authority from various agents of government namely the IRS and Police only to be met with hostility, but mostly silence in their quest for answers.

There are indeed dismissive arguments to Steven's approach notably seeing his method of asking for facts concerning matters of Law to be irrelevant as a popular interpretation goes as follows: that law is not a Matter of Fact and so no facts or evidence beyond the Law existing are needed. On the other hand their efforts once again expose the volatility of the legal paradigm as subject to manipulation and interpretation, and so to be unfit for the operation of a sane and sustainable socioeconomic framework, adding to the argument favouring a NLRBE.

Mark's method is distinctly different from that of other methods examined in this work of sovereignty based Freeman, Lawful Rebellion and Commercial redemption approaches in trying to gain true freedom and independence from Government. One other individual who practices similar is Nathan Fraser, who has stated having tried these methods only ended up 'running into brick walls'.[91],[92],[93]

Where as the Sovereignty movements will try to have government recognize them as sovereign beings through the right legal methods with the resulting expectation of then being acknowledged to no longer be wards of the state, with the right to not contract with government and therefore pay no taxes for example, Nathan's self described form of self-deterministic

[91] http://livefreefm.com/
[92] https://redice.tv/radio-3fourteen/anarchism-and-sovereignty
[93] https://redice.tv/red-ice-radio/the-crumbling-system-of-law-and-authority

'Anarchism' does not recognise government as a legitimte entity whatsoever, merely a fictional entity concoted on self appointed belief as a form of tyranny and violence on the masses to extort taxes, charges and fees etc. through acts and statutes.

The basis to Nathan's philosophy is the upholding of mutual consent in regards to human relations also very much the appraoch of Mark Steven's who subscribe to this view from the much earlier and original philosophies of Lysander Spooner of a self-determining society of mutual contracts and negotiation in trade and services without the need or recognition for federal government jurisdiciton, intervention or interferrence, as well as through the use of a debt free currency.

Both Nathan and Mark resolutely came to doubts on the soveriegn approaches due to the fact of having tried the methods both in and out of court with little to no success or acknowledgement. Nathan having been to court personally close to fourty times using various sovereignty methods such as Affidavits, A4V's (Accepted for Value), Refusal for Cause and Claiming Soverign Jurisdiction none of which were successful.

Why exactly Nathan says for them not to have worked was due to them realizing they didn't correspond with the courts own rules and so found no evidence of being recognized nor respected. They instead have alternatively found success in going the route of getting the court to make its proof of claim of authority and be the one with burden of proof, indeed quite the oposite to the sovereignty approach of trying to present ones proof of clam to being a sovereign. Nathan's strategy in having success with this approach has been due to asking the right questions by studying the court systems own rules of evidence, criminal and civil procedure and understanding how the court system works so as to make the Judge see the fallibility of the system, often they say, with the Judge dismissing or porlonging the case so as for Nathan not to be proven right.

A familiarity if recalled of the Mortgage case with Michael of Bernicia and the double standard hypocracies as witnessed.

BEING THE MAN OR WOMAN

The approach of Karl Lentz is simple in the sense that they have studied and comprehend the legal system in relation to the persona of the STRAWMAN and how it is used to have us contract and transaction with other likewise personas, so as to avoid it. In regards to one's name they take the position that it is their name regardless of any STRAWMAN associations while in event of having to deal with personas for whatever legal reason for whatever purpose. A hypothetical scenario could be a court summons from the tax department, the key to their approach is to do so as a man or women and to likewise address those (claimant or plaintiff) making a claim against you as a man or women and not their occupational title i.e. the persona, while refusing to deal with any lawyer or legal representative. If you were next to appear at the court expecting a man or women as the claimant or plaintiff you would likewise win by default knowing they aren't and indeed can't appear only doing so as the persona of a commercial/legal entity such as the tax department. You then would offer remedy to any verified claims, again to the man or women you may have been dealing with inside the tax department being the only one with firsthand knowledge behind any claim or application of which there again won't be for the same reason, so you again win by default.

Lentz is aware also that going to court should be a last resort, in fact a number of those researched are aware of this. One should never need to go to court as one only need do so if there is controversy to be argued and claims to be made, with first settling any hint of claim or dispute with another party on paper being a basic summation. Also the case that any relevant mail such as a court summons one may receive will always be to the persona and to write on or apply a label saying " Addressee Not Recognized" before posting it back so as to avoid what is commonly known as joinder as an offer to contract with your persona. Lentz has this method summarized as thus: Never have the name of a man or women making the claimant unless it is a man or woman making the claim.

CRADLE TO GRAVE

The final subject to follow having been left until last for the very reason that it may well be the most controversial, but as plausible evidence and explanations will help substantiate, be a pinnacle in our discoveries and understandings of the legal reality concerning us all; of our very existence as a race, as communities, families and individuals. That through its revelations in many ways may have come full circle in this work. As we know understand, all legal and commercial activities operate on the basis of credit and securities through the means of legalization, registration, certification, securitization and general deposit. Again, we don't have to cry conspiracy to understand why those powers of the time in the 1930s as their successors do now colluded to intentionally alter the socioeconomic fabric of the west and most certainly the rest of the world as a consequence, without divulging this to the public let alone by referendum.

It is Perhaps, as demonstrated with the Vatican as well monarchical, governmental and financial powers through some form of right while having come to regard themselves as custodians of law and socioeconomic order for the greater good of the masses choose not to disclose such operations, while through the election and party system process have grown complacent in their positions, often proving time and again an arrogance and air of superiority to those they claim to represent, while hiding behind a wall of bureaucracy and administration resulting in pseudo-democratic and plutocratic tyranny underlined by the control mechanism of the legal reality framework.

As a final note on the soverignty movement, the following correlates to a widely held awarness of there being a possible Trust[94] generated as part of the following process accessible only to State powers of a given territory

---

[94] Your Birth Certificate Sold on Security Exchange PART 1

https://www.youtube.com/watch?v=mU6ZAJAiYOk

as beneficiaries with claims meanwhile having been made for it possible to access for personal benefit are however still largely unproven or verified due to accounts given being too few and far between, with some even debunking it entirely. Despite being the case the following account describes the process and indeed how it may be real entirely.

THE BIRTH CERTIFICATE - A BOND FOR LIFE?

The following consists of information that substantiate the turning of the Birth Certificate into a securitized instrument, followed by an account of how despite being allegedly true is inaccessible to the originator (the human being) due to the legal framework in place and finally so as to be comprehensive a debunking of any evidence of maliciousness of the legal reality toward the health and prosperity of humanity.

In a brief but informative article posted in 2012 by a member by the name of Bill of online chat group Reclaim Your Securities, a Yahoo Group' under the topic heading they gave 'The Uniform Securitization Scheme (the Birth Scam): The universal boilerplate securities transaction blueprint that governs your commercial life. They detail the series of transactions that comprise of what they deem 'the birth scam' of how government (in this case the U.S) convert the birth of a child into a financial asset to underwrite the public debt and the issuance of fiat currency. They begin with acknowledging the fact that the U.S Government is a corporation as defined in Section 3002 of the Judiciary Code. It is from here we can begin to understand the nature of its operations and the validation of the Birth Certificate being traded on the stock market as much as any other security and explain just why they dub it to be part of The Uniform Securitization Scheme where they explain –

> "The Uniform Securitization Scheme which runs invisibly as the operational schematic that underlines all public events be it the birth of a baby, the issuance of currency, economic "bailouts", a court case, a purchase, a loan, a mortgage or a real estate transaction. Without your awareness, virtually every event of your life which involves a public institution has been covertly superimposed on the underlying Uniform Securitization Scheme. - To understand the Uniform Securitization Scheme is to understand the commercial world around you, and the banks, government agencies and Courts that seek to control your life."

A plausible evidence to begin believing and understanding the possibility that the birth certificate could in any way have commodity value again can be traced back to the events of the 1930s, where the deliberate process was set in place to make currency fiat and with it a world of credit and securities backed by faith and the future pledge by governments to the banking powers to pay back public debts through the labours of the citizenry along with it. Suddenly that analogy from The Matrix of human batteries begins to make sense, the dangers and implications of constitution and citizenship and all the more reason to question the jurisdiction of government over oneself as done by Mark Stevens.

The author next describes the process for how the Birth Certificate becomes an instrument of securitization (within the U.S at least) as a pledge of future performance. Most commonly the right foot of the baby is used to make an impression on the hospital birth record providing public testimony of the birth on the continent and status as part of the beginning of that human's surety for the national debt with its future labours as will be paid by the STRAWMAN in taxes through this registration.

The hospital birth record is then delivered to the incorporated County where the transmitting of that human's pledge into the legal system takes place and the opening of an account in their name. As with any asset the incorporate County as the receiving institution must open an account in the County's books and log it in as to leverage future securities. This the author further describes it to be the "boilerplate event" meaning from then on any bank, court, corporation or government institution seeking to assess the owner of a portion of the public debt and tap into your estate[95] to pay the assessment.

In the instance of a registration process in the U.S the author demonstrates this with the following –

> "The County birth account is assigned a number in the format: 123-45-654321 with the first number group identifying the corporate state, second the year of delivery and third group the transaction."

---

[95] As with all commercial and financial transaction frameworks as previously examined estate refers to being that of a Trust.

The registrar then records the hospital birth record in the account as a general deposit as how the Government takes title to the funds (future labor/commercial energy) the same way a bank takes title to a deposit when using a bank's 'Pay to Order' endorsement stamp used for checks for paying to the bank. The author describes this as a 'material alternation' and in the case of the U.S one made under the UCC [96] where a new security is then made by the bank for its own purposes while disguising this acquisition in issuing credit to an account, the government doing much the same. The record is then placed in a vault at city hall, county seat or subsidiary as Vital Records. For those still skeptical the author invites U.S readers to examine their own Birth Certificates alongside a typical stock or bond certificate while reading up on the definition of securities in 'Section 78c of Title 15 of United States Code (subparagraph (a)(10))'.

---

[96] Uniform Commercial Code.

LEGALISING THE ESTATE

After these initial stages the legalization process next happens. This begins by depositing the security future pledge into a public account and hence convert it into a public estate to act as the surety for a person's portion of the public debt, as essentially an insurance to underwrite the public debt. The registrar certifies the deposit of the pledge by issuing a Certificate of Live Birth also known as the long-form identifying the child, parents, date of birth and date of certification.

The author mentions also the definition of a Certified Security from Section 8-102(a)(4) of the UCC to be 'A security that is represented by a certificate' relevant to how certification is used to launder credit applications (such as credit cards, loans and mortgages) into an asset to be sold to investors by banks. The same process is taking place with the issuing of the Certificate by the Registrar, which turns the hospital birth record into a certified security and the County as the depository institution in place of a bank that takes title to the funds to be further regarded as an asset for use as tangible funds in various public accounts. It is here the author males mention of the significance of the inverted and manipulated operations of relationship having taken place between government and the public as demonstrated with the trust triangle diagrams featured earlier where the obligation to perform is transferred from public officials sworn to act as trustees of the public trust to the STRAWMAN trough this legalizing process.

The Secretary of the Treasury is then notified of the pledge by the transmission of a certified copy of the pledge certificate or electronic record of the County deposit, which fully legitimizes and activates the account.

A recap of the process can be given as follows:

- Create the account
- Make a general deposit
- Certificate the asset
- Issue derivative securities

The Secretary delegates then open an account identified by a previously assigned birth certificate number to issue securities against the estate. The pledge represented by the Certificate of live Birth is deposited to provide the funds against which future securities will be issued. Every potential indictment, citation, bill, bond, charging instrument, complaint, summons, arrest warrant, promissory note, assessment and mortgage is then taken from this fund, this is otherwise known as being 'pre-paid' in research circles as the long form Certificate of Live Birth representing the security future pledge of future labor. If the reader hasn't yet thought of the question, if one can track down and access this account there have indeed been those to try and do so known by the term 'Commercial Redemption' which we'll get to shortly.

CREATION OF THE TRUST

As a main purpose of a Trust is to transfer property consequently creates a relationship in which the recipient (trustee) has an obligation to perform certain functions as part of the conveyance of that property, creating what is called the Birth Trust. This original pledge signified by the original birth number assigned by the County registrar can represent a whole variety of accounts, trusts, securities and certificates.

Like any bond the birth bond represents evidence of debt in relation to surety being in this case the public debt, as previously examined. The profiteering off of the bond begins with it being traded for money, which is placed into circulation by the Federal Reserve through the Treasury. The bond is transmitted by the Federal Reserve to 'The Depository Trust Company' (DTC) based in New York and placed in safe keeping to be used in the further re-issuing of a number of derivative securities written against the pledge of the bond.

If recall from our earlier examination of the mortgage securitization process of how the owner (originator) of the assets for investors to trade upon being the sponsor pool of low to middle income residential mortgage payers, similarly in this case can a creditor register a security interest against the owner of the bond, where the DTC as published in their own operational agreements state that beneficiaries are synonymous with ownership despite a beneficiary of a trust as one meant to have the right to enjoy the fruits of the security be demoted to owner, [97] with only the right to order the sale of the security to a next owner.

Let alone the fact that the owner being remotely aware of this whole process, the DTC also make profits on the sale of bonds as holder of the securities. To add insult to injury the party of 'Direct Participant' i.e. the Federal Reserve are also credited with the value of the security allowing for increased net worth on the security and borrow against its as a source of credit to lend double to triple its valued amount.

THE SOCIAL SECURITY BOND

Again in the instance of the U.S the Treasury issues a further security against the pledge in what is called a 'Master Social Security Bond' used as a 'vessel' to transmit public debt. This is done by once again having the originator become surety of their portion of public debt by activating their social security account and receive a (SSN) Social Security Number, while in the process the Treasury authorizes the opening of an account to receive the SS bond to leverage securities with the assigned SSN number in order to identify derivative bonds issued from the account against the estate (pledge).

There again the Master Social Security Bond' creates a trust relationship just as with the birth bond as yet another manifestation of debt that public officials use for their public projects where the Treasury through the IRS rightly should act as trustee of record, but yet again the inversion and manipulation of the trust triangle in place makes the Treasury beneficiary and the STRAWMAN account the trustee and so expected (to a clueless and hapless public) perform all a trustees duties while continuing to be treated as

---

[97] The party liable for all debts and injuries caused by the security

a vehicle for transmitting public debt assessments to the estate of the Master Social Security Bond' for the liability.

The most obvious clue to this relationship is the coercion of paying taxes to continually bolster national debt. The powers that be can't allow nor risk disclosing the truth to the public of this set up for obvious reasons of institutional preservation and potential social breakdown.

BREAKING THE BOND

This stranglehold of debt slavery the author contests can be reversed and the trust triangle restored if enough public awareness and action were made in claiming authorization of and using the SS estate to transmit funds to the rightful party. Such actions have indeed been taken by a number of people and a practicing counter culture does exist particularly in the U.S but as the following account will show proves to be no silver bullet.

COMMERCIAL REDEMPTION

This evidence of securitization and practice of the issuing of bonds and establishment of trusts lend plausible credence to the securitization of Birth Certificates from the account and testament of its author. The basic theoretical premise of Commercial Redemption as mentioned briefly is the attempt to take charge of this surety for public debt by obtaining a certified copy of ones Birth Certificate to be accepted for value (A4V) in all commercial dealings. In the case of the U.S this would be achieved what they describe as becoming a first-secured creditor and the registering of that claim with the Secretary-of-State under the UCC publicly.

Note the word theoretical, as author of the article Commercial Redemption Rejected as Valueless as featured on the website lawfulpath.com. Gregory Allen having had their share of trial and error with this process have resolutely come to describe it to be so, doing so for a number of reasons of which they point out.

Basing on what we now know of the trust process regarding title of ownership etc. what a Birth Certificate was exactly, being a document that certifies existence of a title, not the title itself was clarified. Secondly, obtaining a certified copy of the Birth Certificate will not prevent another copy being made nor a change in the holder of the title. Obtaining the original they explain is near impossible due to internal bureaucratic barriers of the filing and recording process, further of the fact that the original would likely have been passed on to various titleholders, much similar to a mortgage note. Allen also only say this in theory, as it is still widely debated within research circles whether the Birth Certificate is 100% proven to be used as a securitized instrument and if anyone has title to our bodies and if true would likely instead be perhaps the 'Statement of live birth' or 'Application of Birth-Certificate' that are hard to obtain.

To make this a 100% true and verified matter of fact, or if indeed not, would require a campaign international in scale, if not only national through an organised and comprehensive campaign from all over the world volunteering to investigate this process and report on the findings of what differences or similarities may arise as a result. With the creation of awareness and verification generated from such a campaign would bring conclusive proof, as indeed with all issues raised in this work regarding the legal reality.

More of simply asking questions and critiquing the answers in-line with the principles of an NLRBE are needed urgently if the masses around the world are to be made aware of the ongoing detriments and effects of arrested development the legal reality generates through corporate governance and control and advance the socioeconomic evolution of humanity to that of a NLRBE for the long term health and sustainability of both humanity and the planet.

THE FAUX REALITY?

Why is it considered unusual or unfounded of those who wish to express the right to not acquiesce to the powers that be by their fellow man. There are indeed numerous debunkers and naysayers of the parties we have just examined claiming to have done their research and comprehend the legal framework adequately to acknowledge there to be nothing morally or tacitly wrong or perverse about it, yet still acknowledging the flaws of the institutions who control and administer it.[98] One additional quotation from the same author featuring as a heavy proponent among the online community in debunking these parties concerning the legal reality, they state the following-

> "An infrequently mentioned yet foundational idea promoted by many dissidents is the idea of a prison-without-bars; however, the faux common law advocates pervert this idea to mean that all of us are somehow subject to "admiralty" or "maritime" law, and that somehow the UCC are the "rules" for how to successfully "navigate" the "high seas of commerce.""

This demonstrates an initial ignorance to the extensiveness of indeed this 'prison-without-bars' even on any personal level let alone the greater impact it is having on us as a species and all other life as a consequence as the evidence present in this work abundantly shows. One has to ask, do they not pay taxes, licences, charges and fees or any such method of extortion on their time and labour, are they even aware of extensive institutional malpractices and abuses taking place across the globe to the accord of this system, perpetuating the status quo of wealth and rule divide in its wake. Furthermore, do they berate the parties for having a view of the system they deem unsubstantiated in their refusal to cultivate it, further proof of their ignorance to a wider scope and scale of its history and proof of events, appearing instead to project their own subjective interpretation of the system onto the matter -

---

[98] https://thelastbastille.wordpress.com/2015/05/11/chilling-dissent-how-government-demonizes-americans/

"Then, these same miscreants use genuine adjectives, such as describing something as Orwellian or Kafakaesque in order to illustrate the prevalence of legalese. Although those terms highlight truly observable things, they manipulate this to push for their misconception of an "admiralty/maritime prison-without-bars."

CONCLUSIONS

Those reading this advocating a NLRBE or becoming educated about it perhaps are all too familiar with the berating that accompanies the adoption of an alternative mindset. History shows this most often to be the case with reactions and oppositions coming from establishment cultivators, mostly out of fear; fear of loss, of safety, comfort, ignorance, the unknown or often for the sake of self-aggrandizement and ego.

Those working to find alternatives within the legal reality will resolutely come to the understanding as a flawed process if seeking any major evolutionary socioeconomic change. There are indeed small everyday victories and progresses being made, such as the work of Mark Stevens of the jurisdictional argument effective of its simplicity[99] as well the financial arena with exposing the fraud of banking, notably residential mortgages. [100]

Yet ultimately an evolution away from the current syste of things is the right course of action, of which an NLRBE can offer.

---

[99] https://www.youtube.com/watch?v=jww4xyP8IGw
[100] https://www.youtube.com/watch?v=ZG8E5YQtPSo&feature=youtu.be

FUTURE POSSIBILITIES FOR A NLRBE?
WITHIN THE LEGAL REALITY

By continuing to ask the right questions and expose the frauds of the system, in turn exposing its inadequacies and contradictions will help evidently bring humanity ever closer to a NLRBE, but what of the present and near future? Does the legal reality hold anything for The Zeitgeist Movement and others similar, is there anything that can be utilized to bring humanity one step closer to a NLRBE? Some activists such as Michael of Bernicia see remedy from modern tyrannical plutocracy in looking to higher laws of international human and indigenous rights to establish rights of land and the cultivation of truly humane societies.[101]

The properties of Trust law could prove useful to hold assets in safekeeping. If, hypothetically speaking, the event ever arose that a movement or project such as The Zeitgeist Movement or The Venus Project ever grew to an adequate size to establish land holdings to develop and cultivate a NLRBE type infrastructure to any scale or degree, could be kept within the Trust for security and use by successive generations as is common practice with many other institutions and parties such as charitable foundations and religions around the world and a plausible utilization of the most beneficial aspects of this system in helping establish the roots of a NLRBE.

In conclusion perhaps most hopefully technological and scientific developments will be enough to make the legal reality a relic of the past it belongs to, but for now we can help take what we know and apply in avoiding that well-worn but most familiar of statements: Those who don't know their history, are doomed to repeat it.

---

[101] http://self-realisation.com/podcast/wake-the-feck-up-podcast-008-the-case-for-sovereign-independence/

THE LEGAL REALITY OVERVIEW

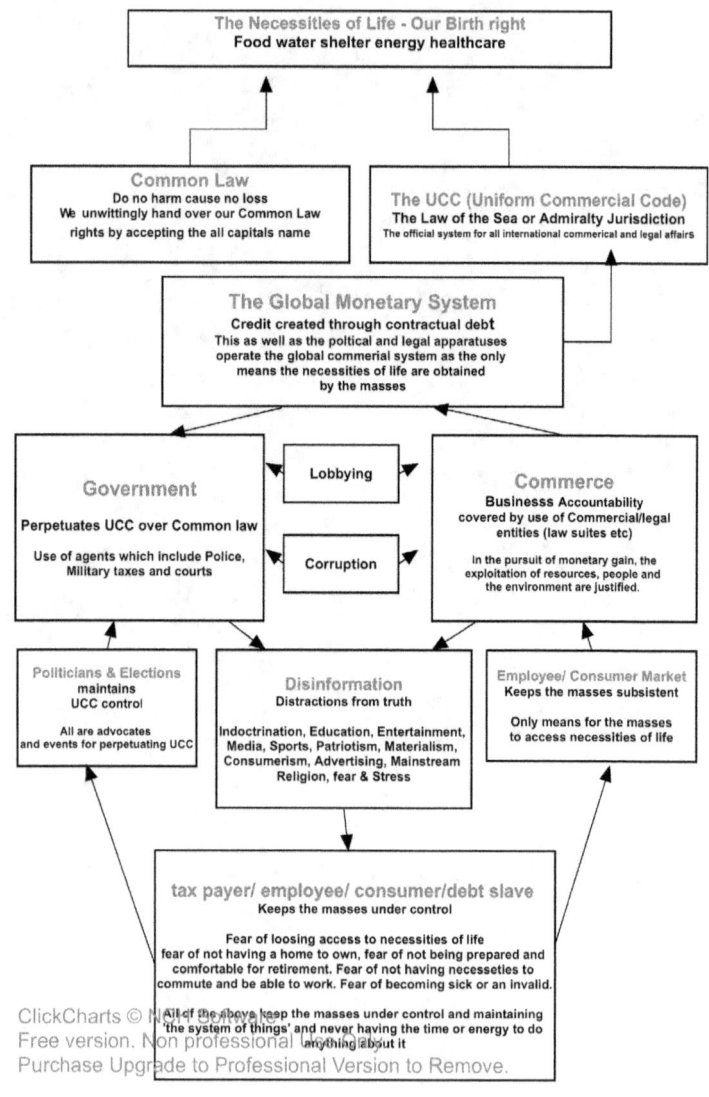

The Necessities of Life - Our Birth right
Food water shelter energy healthcare

Common Law
Do no harm cause no loss
We unwittingly hand over our Common Law
rights by accepting the all capitals name

The UCC (Uniform Commercial Code)
The Law of the Sea or Admiralty Jurisdiction
The official system for all international commerical and legal affairs

The Global Monetary System
Credit created through contractual debt
This as well as the poltical and legal apparatuses
operate the global commerial system as the only
means the necessities of life are obtained
by the masses

Government
Perpetuates UCC over Common law
Use of agents which include Police,
Military taxes and courts

Lobbying

Corruption

Commerce
Business Accountability
covered by use of Commercial/legal
entities (law suites etc)
In the pursuit of monetary gain, the
exploitation of resources, people and
the environment are justified.

Politicians & Elections
maintains
UCC control
All are advocates
and events for perpetuating UCC

Disinformation
Distractions from truth
Indoctrination, Education, Entertainment,
Media, Sports, Patriotism, Materialism,
Consumerism, Advertising, Mainstream
Religion, fear & Stress

Employee/ Consumer Market
Keeps the masses subsistent
Only means for the masses
to access necessities of life

tax payer/ employee/ consumer/debt slave
Keeps the masses under control
Fear of loosing access to necessities of life
fear of not having a home to own, fear of not being prepared and
comfortable for retirement. Fear of not having necesseties to
commute and be able to work. Fear of becoming sick or an invalid.
All of the above keep the masses under control and maintaining
'the system of things' and never having the time or energy to do
anything about it

FURTHER RESOURCES

For more research documents, web links,
book recommends and educational videos

visit

roadblocksnlrbe.weebly.com

NOTES